On Good Friday evening, April 14, 1865, President Abraham Lincoln sat in his box at Ford's Theater in Washington, D.C. He was virtually unguarded and almost a posed target for assassination. The policeman guarding the outer door had disappeared. No soldiers were on duty in the theater. No Secret Service agents were anywhere in the house. At a little after 10:00 that evening, while watching a performance of *Our American Cousin,* he was shot by the actor John Wilkes Booth. Carried unconscious across the street, he died about 7:30 the next morning. A nation was shocked. The authorities investigating the brutal murder were perplexed and confused. At length, a strange web of conspiracy was uncovered, and the guilty were either hanged or imprisoned. Yet an eerie aura of mystery still persists about the Lincoln murder case that cannot be dispelled even today.

PRINCIPALS

ABRAHAM LINCOLN, sixteenth President of the United States.

EDWIN M. STANTON, Lincoln's Secretary of War.

WILLIAM H. SEWARD, Lincoln's Secretary of State.

ANDREW JOHNSON, Vice-President of the United States, later seventeenth President.

GENERAL LAFAYETTE C. BAKER, Chief of Federal Secret Service, in charge of the manhunt for Lincoln's assassin and conspiracy accomplices.

JOHN WILKES BOOTH, noted stage star, matinee idol, Confederate secret agent, and Secession zealot who assassinated President Lincoln in Ford's Theater.

MARY EUGENIA SURRATT, widow, Southern partisan and probable underground supporter; accused of operating Washington boardinghouse that served as "the nest where the egg was hatched."

JOHN H. SURRATT, son of Widow Surratt; Confederate secret agent.

LEWIS T. POWELL (alias Paine, Hull, Wood, Kincheloe), Confederate saboteur assigned to murder Secretary Seward.

DAVID E. HEROLD, Booth associate and getaway guide.

GEORGE ATZERODT, SAMUEL ARNOLD, MICHAEL O'LAUGHLIN, NED SPANGLER, members of Booth's underground crew.

DR. SAMUEL A. MUDD, country physician, Southern partisan who set the fugitive assassin's broken leg.

GARRETT FAMILY, residents of Virginia farm where Booth was shot.

John Wilkes Booth leaps from the President's box in Ford's Theater after shooting Abraham Lincoln. Catching his spur in the flag draped before the presidential box, the assassin broke his leg when he landed on the stage below. (National Archives)

The Lincoln Assassination, April 14, 1865

by Theodore Roscoe

Investigation of a President's Murder Uncovers a Web of Conspiracy

ILLUSTRATED WITH PRINTS AND PHOTOGRAPHS

FRANKLIN WATTS, INC.
845 Third Avenue, New York, N.Y. 10022

The authors and publisher of the Focus Books wish to acknowledge the helpful editorial suggestions of Professor Richard B. Morris.

Contents

Ford's Theater on Tenth Street in Washington, D.C., scene of the Lincoln assassination. Photograph was taken shortly after the murder. Note the mourning bands draped outside the building. (Library of Congress)

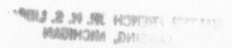

Target for Murder

On Good Friday evening, April 14, 1865, Abraham Lincoln, President of the United States, sat in a box in Ford's Theater in the heart of the nation's capital, posed as a target for assassination. The young officer sitting as a guest in the State Box with him was unarmed. The policeman ordered to guard the outer door had disappeared. There were no soldiers on duty in the theater; no horse guards posted at the entrance or stage door; no military police, Special Officers, or Federal Secret Service agents anywhere in the house.

Under the circumstances — the curtain coming down on a savage civil war; Washington seething with excitement; the District infested with enemy parolees, spies, and saboteurs, some of whom were known to be nesting within a stone's throw of the Tenth Street playhouse — under these circumstances, the situation at Ford's Theater seems incredible. Lincoln was exposed in the stage box like someone placed in a chair before the target of a rifle range. . . .

Abraham Lincoln had been marked for murder the day he was elected president. In the American South, proslavery forces raged at mention of his name. William Russell, London *Times* correspondent, reported that Southern cities teemed with firebrand orators, pistol-waving racists, plug-uglies, and bullies calling for war against "Old Abe."

In Mobile, Alabama, that winter, a rabid mob lynched a man from the U.S.S. *Brooklyn*. In Montgomery a gunman on a platform brandished a rifle and promised to slay the abolition-lover bound for the White House. In New Orleans, Charleston, and Richmond the press pronounced Lincoln anathema. Threatening letters and baleful maledictions swamped Lincoln's mail. Nor was it reassuring to realize that some of the writers were obviously insane.

Lincoln's friend Ward Lamon was worried about him in February, 1861, when the President-elect left Springfield, Illinois, for Washington.

And before the Lincoln party reached New York alarming word came from Boston social worker Dorothea Dix, who warned that enemies planned to waylay the Lincoln train in Baltimore. Railroad magnate Samuel Felton had already hired Chicago detective Allan Pinkerton to guard the right-of-way. Hastening to Baltimore, Pinkerton uncovered a sinister plot.

He traced it to the Barnum Hotel, rendezvous for such self-styled heroes as the "Palmetto Guards" and the "Knights of the Golden Circle" — fraternities devoted to chauvinistic balderdash and racism. A leader there was the hotel barber, Cipriano Fernandina, a Charlestonian advocate of anarchy and secession. Shadowing him, Pinkerton learned that an underground gang had drawn ballots to determine who would assassinate Lincoln at the Calvert Street Depot. So Lincoln's schedule was changed at Philadelphia. A Pinkerton agent, Mrs. Kate Warne, guarded the door to Lincoln's car, six-shooter under her cloak. Other guards and Ward Lamon sat close at hand. The train ride through Baltimore proved uneventful. But the menace continued to hover over Lincoln.

Of course, the danger increased after the Civil War exploded in April, 1861. Washington teemed with Rebel secret agents and saboteurs. The authorities received dire warnings that Lincoln would be murdered in 1862.

In the summer of 1863 Federal intelligence agents learned that a secret society of Virginia slave barons was raising a fund for Lincoln's assassination. In the North, anti-Lincoln "Knights" and other "Copperheads" uttered blood oaths, vowing to kill him.

One day a female saboteur disguised in black mourning clothes visited the White House. Raising her veil, she tried to infect Lincoln with smallpox by kissing him. Or so it was reported. The story was officially denied, but Lincoln did in fact suffer an attack of varioloid — a mild case of smallpox.

In March, 1864, the New York *Tribune* published an anonymous letter describing in detail a plot to kidnap Lincoln. The writer told of a back road down through Lower Maryland as the route to be used by the abductors. At Indian Point or at Port Tobacco they would board a boat to

[2]

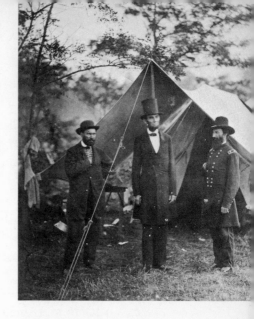

President Abraham Lincoln is shown here during the Civil War with Allan Pinkerton of the Secret Service (left) and General John McClernand. (Library of Congress)

cross the Potomac to Virginia. With relay teams they would then whisk the prize captive on down to Richmond, the Confederate capital.

Union intelligence uncovered evidence that developed into yet another kidnap picture. Lincoln was to be seized during one of his evening strolls to the War Department or to Army headquarters in the Winder Building on Seventeenth Street. Or, if opportunity presented, he might be waylaid when he drove out to the Soldiers' Home. In either case, his captors planned to hide him in the old Van Ness mansion at the foot of Seventeenth — an isolated house surrounded by a high brick wall overlooking the Potomac. The owner of the place, a Colonel Green, had two sons in the Army of Virginia. The house was a station on the Gray underground, used as a spy "letter drop."

The leader of this proposed kidnapping was a Confederate agent named Thomas N. Conrad. He and a Rebel spy named Mountjoy had devised the plan in the winter of 1863. They recruited a coachman named Williams and a hulking fellow called Frizzell for the enterprise. But the scheme collapsed when Lincoln unexpectedly adopted a cavalry escort for his carriage and Conrad realized that the White House must have been forewarned. Still, Conrad himself escaped apprehension. As with the Fernandina gang, he and his band simply vanished underground.

[3]

The cavalry escort had been urged on Lincoln by War Secretary Edwin M. Stanton. The President had already consented to a White House guard consisting of three or four unobtrusive policemen selected from Washington City's Metropolitan Force. But an occasional escort was not enough. In August, 1864, a hidden sniper put a bullet through Lincoln's hat on the road near the Soldiers' Home.

In the autumn of 1864 the Confederates unleashed a campaign to sabotage the North with fire raids, prison breaks, train wrecks, counterfeiting, and germ warfare devised to spread yellow fever. And a Union secret agent in Canada reported the enemy was brewing up a scheme to slay Lincoln.

In December, 1864, a newspaper in Selma, Alabama, published a citizen's offer to assassinate President Lincoln, Secretary Seward, and Vice-President Andrew Johnson for one million dollars.

Then in February, 1865, the U.S. War Department was advised that a gang of subversives in Washington planned to assault Lincoln during his second inaugural address. The informant was a government employee, Louis J. Wiechmann. He told his story to Captain D. H. L. Gleason, a

An Eye to
(Ala.)   h   the
vertiseme
One Million Dollar   nted,   we
Peace by the 1st of March.—If the citizens of the Southern Confederacy will
furnish me with the cash, or good secu-
rities for the sum of one million dollars,
I will cause the lives of Abraham Lincoln, William H. Seward and Andrew
Johnson to be taken by the first of March
next. This will give us peace, and sat-
isfy the world that cruel tyrants can not
live in the "land of liberty." If this is
not accomplished nothing will be claimed beyond the sum of fifty thousand dollars, in advance, which is supposed to be
necessary to reach and slaughter the
three villians.

I will give, myself, one thousand dollars towards this patriotic purpose.

Every one wishing to contribute will
address box X, Cahaba, Alabama.   X.
December 1, 1864.

Notice published in Selma, Alabama, offering to slay Abraham Lincoln, William H. Seward, and Andrew Johnson for one million dollars. (National Archives)

War Department officer. Wiechmann named names — matinee idol John Wilkes Booth; spy John Surratt; a secret agent called Paine or the Reverend Wood, and others. Further, Wiechmann gave an address — Mrs. Mary Surratt's boardinghouse (where he lived) at 541 H Street. He said that Mrs. Surratt owned a tavern on a back road in Lower Maryland at a place called Surrattsville, and that this inn was a way station on the Rebel underground to Port Tobacco and Richmond. Wiechmann also said that Mrs. Surratt entertained spies named Gus Howell, a Major Somebody, and a Mrs. Slater, and that her son and Booth were plotting to do away with the President.

Alarmed, Gleason relayed the story to Captain George H. Sharp, Chief of the Bureau of Military Information — Army intelligence headquarters in the War Department. Someone promptly arrested the Rebel spy Howell on his way to Mrs. Surratt's boardinghouse. But nothing more was done.

Late in March an effort was made to ambush the President's carriage near the Soldiers' Home. Fortunately, Lincoln was not in the vehicle. The enemy horsemen fled. Again nothing was done.

On April 5, 1865, Lincoln boarded the U.S. flagship *Malvern* in the James River just below Richmond. The Confederate capital lay under siege, collapsing. While Lincoln was aboard, Union General Edward H. Ripley reported with urgent word for the President. With Ripley was a captured soldier who admitted to serving in the so-called Rains Bureau — a special branch of the Confederate Secret Service. He said he had been assigned to a mission *"aimed at the head of the Yankee government."* He would not — and probably could not — provide further details, but the import remained obvious and ominous.

One night, shortly before his assassination, Lincoln was much disturbed by a sinister dream. He did not attach superstitious meanings to dreams, but this one, in which he seemed to attend his own funeral, depressed him. Probably it echoed recent threats.

A final warning arrived from General James Van Alen who urged Lincoln "for the sake of his friends and the nation" to guard his life and not expose himself to assassination as he did on his trip to Richmond. Lincoln answered this letter on April 14, a short time before he went to the theater. He wrote, "I intend to adopt the advice of my friends and use due precaution. . . ." He thanked Van Alen for support "in the efforts I may make to restore the Union, so as to make it, to use your language, a Union of hearts and hands as well as of States." This was the last letter Lincoln ever wrote.

A later generation of historians, uninformed about the Van Alen letter, came to regard Lincoln as resigned and fatalistic. Yet Lincoln did attempt to exercise caution. On that crucial afternoon, following a cabinet meeting attended by General Grant (who apologized because he and Mrs. Grant would not accept Mrs. Lincoln's invitation to go to the theater that evening), perhaps troubled by Grant's abrupt departure, Lincoln walked over to the War Department to request a special guard at the theater. He asked War Secretary Stanton for the services of Major Thomas T. Eckert, a strapping intelligence officer who, Lincoln himself said, "could bend a poker over his arm."

Informed that Eckert could not be spared, Lincoln in whimsical disbelief went to Eckert's office to ask him in person. But the major had heard Stanton's raspy refusal. So he said he was needed at the code and cipher desk.

Lincoln made no protest, although it seems he had a premonition. *"Do you know,"* he had said to his bodyguard William Crook, as they passed a group of toughs on Pennsylvania Avenue, *"I believe there are men who want to take my life. And I have no doubt they will do it."*

There were. And they did that very evening, when Lincoln went to the theater unprotected. . . .

Who Was Responsible for Lincoln's Safety?

Three top officials were responsible for the Chief Executive's security. These were: Edwin M. Stanton, U.S. Secretary of War; General Lafayette C. Baker, Chief of the U.S. Secret Service, and General Christopher C. Augur, in command of Army forces in the District of Columbia.

As head of the War Department, Stanton ranked high in responsibility. Why, then, did he refuse Lincoln the simple services of husky Major Eckert? Nobody knows. Historian Otto Eisenschiml, researching the last scrap of available information, found that code officer Eckert was not at all busy that evening. In fact, he went home early. And War Secretary Stanton himself went home to an early supper. To this day the Eckert matter remains inexplicable.

Stanton was a strange person. By today's medical standards he would undoubtedly have been pronounced a psychotic. He suffered from chronic asthma, a nerve-crippling affliction. And as a young man he exhibited erratic compulsions. While a student he clerked for several seasons in a Columbus, Ohio, bookstore. There he boarded with a water-cure healer known as a "steam doctor" — a common frontier type — whose house-

Edwin M. Stanton, Secretary of War in Lincoln's Cabinet. (Library of Congress)

hold featured an attractive daughter. One morning, shortly after Stanton departed for work, the girl fell ill. It was cholera. She died that same afternoon, and Stanton came home at suppertime to find her buried. Wildly he rushed to the cemetery, procured a spade, and dug up her body. Afterward he said he feared she had been buried alive by the rough-and-ready local undertakers. While neighbors applauded his clinical concern in the case, no one seemed to observe his manifest lack of interest in the area's other hurriedly buried epidemic victims.

Some years later, when Stanton's little daughter Lucy died, he had her body exhumed and placed in a metal casket, which he kept for months in his bedroom.

When his wife, Mary, died, he kept her nightcap and nightdress in his bed for many weeks, mourning. He spent days in the cemetery, haunting her grave.

After his brother Darwin committed suicide, Stanton wandered about in a state of hysteria. Friends feared he might kill himself. But in time he recovered, and presently a lucrative law career gained him the sobriquet "King of Steubenville," after the Ohio town in which he practiced.

It was during a precedent-setting action — the famous McCormick Reaper Case — that Lincoln and Stanton became acquainted as counsels for the defendant. The "King of Steubenville" had professional status by then; Lincoln was an unknown frontier lawyer. Stanton treated him as though he were a clod and refused to dine with him at their hotel. Once he said, within Lincoln's hearing, that he would not associate with that "long-legged ape." He derided Lincoln's brief as "trash." Humiliated, Lincoln sat on the sidelines while Stanton and another attorney addressed the bench. But Lincoln later told Ralph Waldo Emerson that Stanton's brilliant courtroom performance convinced him he should go home and study more law.

In the 1850's, Stanton again gained national notice out in California, where he untangled land grants, Spanish deeds, and realty taken from the Mexicans. His successful practice eventually took him to Washington, where he served as attorney general in the cabinet of President James Buchanan.

Under Buchanan, Stanton unexpectedly assumed a strong Unionist stand. Yet he disliked Lincoln's election to the Presidency. Stanton pronounced him an "imbecile" and a "giraffe," and derided him in letters to Buchanan using language long since edited out of popular history books. The fact that Lincoln appointed Stanton Secretary of War to replace the inept Simon Cameron has baffled many biographers.

Whatever he might think of Lincoln, Stanton, as war secretary, worked like a steam engine. Wiping up shameful messes of Army procurement graft — defective munitions, sick horses, uniforms that dissolved in the rain — he won himself laurels as "the Mad Incorruptible." Lincoln called him "old Mars."

Yet Stanton also tolerated some shady cotton deals by General Ben Butler's brother and some fast footwork with contracts for friends at home. As for his "old Mars" image, Stanton's strategy would draw much postwar fire, and his snap judgments, flash court-martials, and overbearing demeanor displayed a curiously officious personality. Earlier, as a trial lawyer, his browbeating tactics once evoked from a St. Clairsville clergyman a promise to knock him flat if he again so abused a witness. Devious, domineering, arrogant, two-faced, opportunistic, cowardly, artful, vengeful — these are some of the descriptive adjectives applied by contemporaries and postwar biographers to Edwin M. Stanton. He was a baffling character.

Although Stanton posed as a bulwark of respectability, one of his closest Washington friends was a slippery New York senator named Daniel Sickles, a profligate libertine who shot dead the playboy Philip Barton Key near the gates of the White House. Another dubious friend of Stanton's was William P. Wood, an artisan of sorts, who gained from Stanton the job of warden of the Old Capitol Prison. Long after the war Wood confessed to rigging false evidence for Stanton to use if necessary in the McCormick case.

[9]

Colonel Lafayette C. Baker,
chief of the Federal Secret Service.
(National Archives)

Of similar stamp was Stanton's confidant Colonel Lafayette C. Baker, a former California vigilante. Stanton made him chief of the National Detective Police, a designation changed by Baker to "United States Secret Service." Baker, with his reddish beard and eyes and his reflex reach for the till when reward money entered in — this was the second official responsible for Lincoln's safety.

Hailing from New England, Philadelphia, and points west, Baker had showed up in Washington in the spring of 1861 and had gained a job as a spy in the service of General Winfield Scott. After one or two missions to Richmond — exploits not necessarily believable — he was appointed by Stanton to head the home-front forces of counterespionage.

Baker set up his bureau in the Treasury Building. With Stanton's backing, he built an invisible army of some two thousand secret agents and spread an intelligence network that eventually became the model for Germany's military spy system and the Russian police state. At Stanton's bidding, he broke up a ring flooding the army with "moonshine" whiskey. He also broke up gambling hells, smashed a syndicate dealing in pornographic photographs, and raided the three-thousand-odd vice dens in Washington on lower Pennsylvania and Ohio avenues — a red-light district known as "Hooker's Division" (with apt reference to the troops of General Hooker). These raids had less to do with Union Army morals than the fact that the places raided were infested with Confederate secret agents and Secessionist sympathizers.

Adopting a flag inscribed "Death to Traitors," the energetic Secret Service chief led his cavalry squadron, dubbed "Baker's Raiders," down the roads of Lower Maryland, hounding Rebel partisans in towns like Piscataway, Port Tobacco, and Piney Point. There was nothing wrong with all this, except for the fact that the cinnamon-whiskered Baker somehow acquired a brimstone smell from black-market payoffs and bribe money. His counterespionage net caught a few Rebel spies, but in April of 1865, a group of enemy subversives gathered without interference in the nation's capital. And on April 14, the day of Lincoln's assassination, Lafayette Baker was chasing bounty jumpers and draft evaders in New York City — and enjoying a stay at the Astor House, far from the stage set in Washington, D.C.

General Christopher Augur, the third official responsible for Lincoln's safety, was a plain rule-book soldier. In underground warfare that abided by no rule he was plainly out of his depth.

In any case, no Army intelligence officers, no Federal Secret Service agents, no military police were at Ford's Theater when John Wilkes Booth arrived on the scene. . . .

John Wilkes Booth and Company

Because spy operations and military assassinations were subjects traditionally taboo, for decades Americans were led to believe that Lincoln's assassination was simply the act of a lunatic suddenly gone berserk. Nothing could be further from the truth. John Wilkes Booth was a secret agent who had been long engaged in espionage and so-called blockade-running for the Confederacy. He had confided to his sister, Asia, that he was a spy.

[11]

Two views of John Wilkes Booth. Photos were made in the early 1860's while he was at the peak of his acting career. (National Archives)

And he spoke of the Confederacy as "his country." His band, generally described as a crew of mediocre misfits, contained an experienced secret agent, an adept guerrilla fighter and saboteur, a couple of infantry veterans, and several Rebel partisans who were more than capable of murder. Above ground they were nothing much. But underground, led by an activist with Booth's compelling personality, they made up a lethal and dangerous gang.

Son of Junius Brutus Booth (an actor billed as that day's greatest Shakespearan), John Wilkes was reared in Baltimore and Bel Air, Maryland. The Booth family might be compared to the Barrymores of latter-day fame. The father was a stage patriarch; the eldest brother, Edwin, enjoyed stardom similar to Lionel's, and John Wilkes's matinee-idol popularity was akin to John Barrymore's. But John Wilkes Booth's debut on the stage in Baltimore, when he was seventeen years old, had been a failure. Stung by hooting galleries and barbed critiques, he had turned to waterfront lounging with a friend, Mike O'Laughlin, and to oyster poaching with Ned Spangler, a yard hand at Bel Air.

Two summers later, again "treading the boards," he played Hamlet in Richmond. This time he brought down the house with every performance. Women threw garlands from the audience, screamed when he took a curtain call, fought for his autograph. Enamored of the South (he borrowed a Richmond Grays uniform in order to attend the hanging of John Brown), he played there until February, 1861. That spring he took a Northern booking, which paid more money. But when the guns crashed at Fort Sumter, Booth made a speech in a theater in Albany, New York, praising the Confederate attack as "heroic." The angry audience chased him out of town.

Friends wondered why he did not hurry south to join the Rebel army. He told his sister he needed funds. The stage paid him $500 a week — a fortune compared to the $5 paid a Confederate volunteer. Naturally it seemed more profitable to die every night as Hamlet or Macbeth, rather than expire once and for all as an underpaid Southern soldier. Besides, the South was winning — at first.

But in 1863 the South began to lose. At some time that winter Booth entered the Gray underground. The Confederate Secret Service had become a highly organized, keenly motivated apparatus with spy rings in every large city of the North. One of the geniuses behind this secret invasion force was G. J. Rains, builder of the famous Rains Bureau devoted to secret warfare. Booth performed initially as a "blockade-runner," smuggling quinine and other drugs to the desperately needy Confederates. His profession served as a front for his activities. Playing Southern cities occupied by the Union armies, he showed a pass signed by General Grant.

Booth's espionage activities have yet to be fully uncovered. When

[13]

Richmond collapsed on April 9, 1865, the Confederacy's chiefs destroyed almost all C.S.A. secret records; the Rains Bureau went up in smoke. But documents preserved elsewhere show Booth working in underground apparatus in Montreal, Boston, New York, Philadelphia, Baltimore, and in the South, with a base in Washington, D.C.

In Washington he lived in the National Hotel at Sixth Street and Pennsylvania Avenue, about midway between the White House and the Capitol. His base was a short walk distant — the boardinghouse of Mrs. Mary Eugenia Surratt at 541 H Street.

The House on H Street

Andrew Johnson called the house "the nest where the egg was hatched." Its owner, Mary Eugenia Jenkins Surratt, a widow in her forties and a patriotic Southerner, certainly operated in the Confederate underground.

She was not the only matron to devote secret time and effort to the Stars and Bars. The famed Rose O'Neal Greenhow, Mrs. Philip Philips, Mrs. Ellena Low, Mrs. William Baxley, Mrs. William Hasler, and other ladies of Southern antecedents or persuasion were also engaged in espionage for the Confederacy. The Widow Surratt, however, was hopelessly middle-class, churchgoingly moral, and poor. She was as rigidly conventional as a horsehair sofa. This last trait may have been the influence that led her into dire trouble.

About eleven miles south of Washington in Lower Maryland, the Surratts owned a small crossroads tavern at a place called Surrattsville. A stagecoach stop on the pike to Port Tobacco, Chapel Hill, and Leonardtown, the tavern became rundown when war ruined the meager business in the locality. Mrs. Surratt was widowed, with two draft-age sons and a daughter to worry about. When her eldest boy went to Texas she procured the local postmastership for her son John. The post office happened

[14]

Mrs. Surratt's boardinghouse on H Street in Washington, D.C.—"the nest where the egg was hatched." (Courtesy Oldroyd Museum)

Mary Eugenia Jenkins Surratt, the notorious widow of the dark underground. (National Archives)

to be in her tavern. It made a perfect letter drop and outpost for Rebel secret agents operating in the Washington area and became a key way station on the Confederate underground that extended from Richmond to Montreal, Canada. (See map on page 46.)

Coming up through Bowling Green, Virginia, the Gray underground agents jumped the Potomac at Port Tobacco, followed the northbound

[15]

road through Surrattsville to Washington, and thence went via Baltimore, New York City, and St. Albans, Vermont, to Montreal. As the Union Navy's ironclad blockade sealed off the South's seaboard, closing the Atlantic and Gulf ports to ocean shipping, this overland "blockade run" by which Gray secret agents could forward overseas or receive important diplomatic dispatches was increasingly vital to the Confederacy. John Surratt became such a blockade-runner on this clandestine route to New York and Montreal, Canada, where the Confederacy maintained a secret base.

In the autumn of 1864, Mrs. Surratt rented her tavern to an impoverished neighbor, John Lloyd, and moved into the three-story house at 541 (now 604) H Street, Washington. Ostensibly to pay for her living expenses, she took in lodgers — a young couple named Holohan; a niece, Appollonia Deane; and Louis Wiechmann, a former classmate of John's from the Catholic seminary up-country. In addition, Mrs. Surratt's daughter Annie and a friend, Honora Fitzpatrick, lived there.

An early caller at the house was John Wilkes Booth, who had been playing at Ford's Theater four blocks away. In fact, Booth became a frequent visitor. And Mrs. Surratt's defenders would later have a hard time trying to explain why a celebrated stage star spent evenings at her modest house when he could have gone to his choice of Washington soirees, or to his Titian-haired mistress, Ella Turner, at the National Hotel. At any rate, he posed as a personal friend of John Surratt's.

Also to the house on H Street came a grubby little German who boarded there for a week in December, 1864. This was George Andrew Atzerodt, whom John Surratt called "Old Plug Tobacco." Atzerodt was a roustabout carriage painter from Port Tobacco. Mrs. Surratt may or may not have known him for an underground boatman who ferried blockade-runners across the Potomac.

Another temporary roomer was a massive six-footer with a sulky boyish face that did not go with the name he gave: the Reverend Wood. To Louis Wiechmann, who saw him move in, "Wood" later confided that his name was "Paine." This was really Lewis Thornton Powell, a Florida product of the Tallahassee area, son of a Baptist preacher. A hard-

[16]

George A. Atzerodt, one of the conspirators in the Lincoln murder plot. (Library of Congress)

Lewis Thornton Powell, alias Lewis Paine, the Reverend Wood, Mr. Kincheloe, and many other assumed names. Paine is shown here under guard after his butchery at the Seward household. (Library of Congress)

shell fundamentalist and rabid racist, he was early in Confederate uniform — the type who relished the sadistic humor of "Sut Luvingood" and drank anti-Union blood oaths from a Yankee skull.

Booth had recruited Powell in Richmond in 1863. As Paine, this young Confederate soldier had been captured at Gettysburg and paroled in Baltimore. He broke parole and left the city after nearly kicking a Negro housemaid to death (he said she was "insolent"). Vowing to avenge his two brothers killed at Stone River, Paine went "scouting" for Mosby's guerrillas. In the autumn of 1864 he made contact with Booth at Barnum's Hotel. He wore a clergyman's costume when he visited Mrs. Surratt's in Washington, but he told Wiechmann he worked for a Baltimore merchant named Parr. Actually, Lewis Thornton Powell Paine was a killer awaiting his mission.

Still another visitor at the H Street house was David Herold. A drugstore errand boy who lived near Navy Yard Bridge on the Anacostia River with his mother and seven sisters, Herold called himself a professional "quail hunter." It was said he was stagestruck and had formed an attachment for Booth, who manipulated him like a puppet on strings. But Wiechmann remembered meeting Herold in the spring of 1863 at the

[18]

Michael O'Laughlin, boyhood chum of Booth's, is shown here after his capture. Note handcuffs. (Library of Congress)

tavern in Surrattsville. It seemed, too, that Herold and John Surratt often hunted the backwoods and swamps of Lower Maryland together.

Two others who may have called at Mrs. Surratt's boardinghouse were Booth's schoolboy chum from Baltimore, Michael O'Laughlin, and a former classmate from Catonsville, Samuel Bland Arnold. Presumably dismissed from the Confederate Army as an incompetent, O'Laughlin may have been ordered into civilian garb to serve with Booth — such orders were not uncommon in the Confederate Secret Service. Similarly, Sam Arnold, reputedly a Rebel Army deserter, may have been operating

Samuel B. Arnold.
(Library of Congress)

Ned Spangler.
(Library of Congress)

with the Rains Bureau. All of them Barnum's Hotel habitués, these Baltimoreans were early in the game with Booth.

Last and least of Booth's Washington accomplices was Ned Spangler, a Bel Air handyman and in 1865 a stagehand at Ford's. A social cut below the others, Spangler apparently never joined them in roistering about the capital with the stage star. Nor did Booth associate with other underground operatives at Mrs. Surratt's house — her friend Augustus Howell, a certain Major Banon, and a mysterious Mrs. Slater. Probably they were in clandestine touch. John Surratt made several furtive blockade-runs with pretty Mrs. Slater.

In August, 1864, a sinister message was found scratched on the windowpane of a room in a hotel in Meadville, Pennsylvania. It read: *"Abe Lincoln Departed this Life August 13, 1864, by the effect of poison."* It appeared that John Wilkes Booth had been in the hotel the night before this defacement was found. Whether or not it was the actor's handiwork remains a moot question. Booth confided to his diary that "capture" engrossed him that summer. By that he meant Lincoln's abduction.

Apparently he borrowed and adapted the original Conrad-Mountjoy kidnap operation. Typical gallery player that he was, however, he wanted to seize Lincoln in a theater for dramatic effect. What a show! Pull it off, and his name would blaze for all time on the marquee of history!

Booth launched two kidnap attempts that failed miserably. In January, 1865, he planned to seize Lincoln at Ford's Theater during a performance of *Jack Cade*. Booth arranged for someone (Spangler?) to shut off the main gas valve and pitch the house into darkness. With John Surratt, Paine, and the boys from Baltimore, all heavily armed, he proposed to burst into the State Box, truss up the President, throw him to the stage, and rush him out back where Herold waited at the stage door with an express wagon. By relay, fast teams were to carry the captive to Port Tobacco where Atzerodt would have a ready barge. Once across the Potomac, the run to Richmond would be easy. With everything set to go, the enterprise fell through because of bad weather. A snowstorm blanketed Washington; Lincoln stayed home from the theater.

[20]

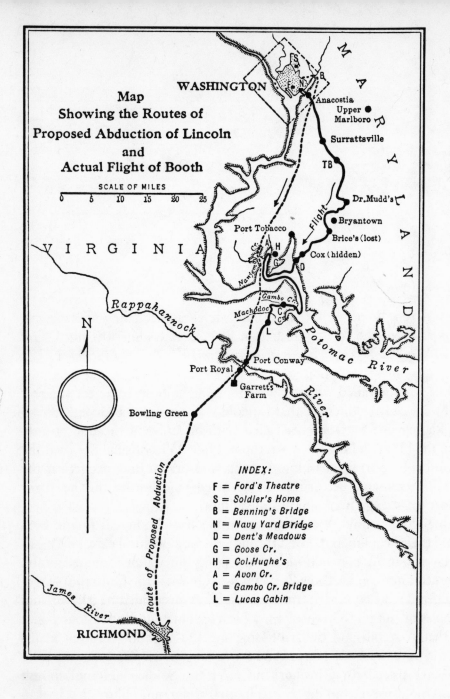

Map
Showing the Routes of
Proposed Abduction of Lincoln
and
Actual Flight of Booth

SCALE OF MILES

0   5   10   15   20   25

WASHINGTON

M A R Y L A N D

Anacostia
Upper Marlboro

Surrattsville

TB

Dr. Mudd's

Bryantown

Brice's (lost)

Cox (hidden)

Port Tobacco

V I R G I N I A

D

Rappahannock

Gambo Cr.

Machodoc

C

L

N

Port Conway

Port Royal

Garrett's Farm

Bowling Green

Potomac River

River

James River

RICHMOND

Route of Proposed Abduction

INDEX:

F = Ford's Theatre
S = Soldier's Home
B = Benning's Bridge
N = Navy Yard Bridge
D = Dent's Meadows
G = Goose Cr.
H = Col. Hughe's
A = Avon Cr.
C = Gambo Cr. Bridge
L = Lucas Cabin

Louis Wiechmann. (Author's collection)

In March, Booth sent O'Laughlin a telegram signaling another try. Having assumed the role of oil baron, he concocted lingo to suit: *"Get word to Sam. Come on, with or without him, Wednesday morning. We sell that day sure. Don't fail."*

The attempt failed when Booth sprang his ambush trap near the Soldiers' Home only to discover that Lincoln was not in the presidential carriage. Raging in frustration, he faded with his crew in the underbrush. Back in the H Street house that afternoon Louis Wiechmann glimpsed the actor and John Surratt gnashing, cursing, and brandishing daggers at the ceiling. This closeted performance convinced Wiechmann that he ought to report the strange household to the authorities.

One would think Wiechmann need not have bothered. Booth, Surratt, and their henchmen traipsed through the fleshpots and cafés of Washington like so many conventioneers on a spree. They dined, drank noisily, and argued loudly in Lichau's Restaurant, Rullman's, the Canterbury Music Hall, and a dozen other public places. They pretended to talk oil, and Booth was in fact up to his neck in wildcat speculation. But anyone could guess that Atzerodt and the stable-smelling O'Laughlin were not investors. Nor were the seedy Herold and the sulking Lewis Paine. Sam Arnold might have passed for a broker, but after the Soldiers' Home ambush fiasco, Arnold wasn't buying any. The two abduction failures led him to

[22]

write Booth a letter advising him to defer another attempt until he saw how things went in Richmond.

Did Booth receive a signal from Richmond? Early in April John Surratt went down to the Confederate capital with Mrs. Slater. He returned with a purse of gold pieces, told friends the South was disintegrating, and then went home to inform his mother he was going to Montreal. With Lewis Paine, Booth listened to Lincoln on the night of April 11. Speaking from a White House window, the President told a cheering throng of Lee's surrender and declared his hope that Negroes would soon be given the vote. According to Paine, Booth had snarled, "That is the last speech *he* will ever make!"

Yet the incentive for murder could have been money. Booth had not played a role since his brief appearance in *Pescara* and a Shakespearean benefit with his brothers Edwin and Junius Brutus in New York the previous November. He was saddled with debts, and he had squandered a bank account on lady friends, including a mistress, a secret fiancée, and a damsel he may or may not have married in Cos Cob. His oil shares had turned to water. And he had been forced to sell a carriage rig and some theatrical regalia to pay his current expenses. With a possible king's ransom promised for Lincoln's assassination, who could say gold was not a most compelling incentive?

During the second week of April, 1865, Booth gathered his band around him. Atzerodt came up from Port Tobacco. Lewis Paine, as "Mr. Kincheloe," signed in at a hotel on Ninth and F Street. Surratt and Herold lurked at hand. Arnold, however, had dropped out. On the thirteenth Booth wired O'Laughlin: *Don't fear to neglect your business. You had better come at once.*

Word was that Lincoln planned to see a play on the night of April 14.

Tragedy at Ford's Theater

About 11:30 A.M. on Good Friday, Booth sauntered up Tenth Street to Ford's Theater, ostensibly to get mail held for him there. Theater manager Henry Clay Ford nudged a bystander. Here came the handsomest man in Washington. Ford handed Booth several letters. Lingering for a minute, Booth noticed that the State Box was being prepared for occupancy. To Booth's question, Ford said yes, that night the President was expected to attend a special performance — Laura Keene in *Our American Cousin*.

Booth had anticipated Glover's Theater. Masking surprise, he glanced casually at his mail. Thomas Raybold in the ticket office heard the actor utter an explosive laugh. Presently Booth reentered the playhouse. He knew every nook and cranny of the house and also every line in the stale old comedy scheduled for that evening.

Inside, he studied the set. There came a moment in act three, scene two, where a comic dowager, Mrs. Mountchessington (played by Mrs. H. Muzzy), bawled out Yankee rube Asa Trenchard (Harry Hawk) and then swept offstage. Whereupon Trenchard, alone on stage, called after her, *"Don't know the manners of good society, eh? Wal, I know enough to turn you inside out, you sockdologizing old mantrap!"* It was a line calculated to please Lincoln. Invariably it brought down the house. The timing — the yokel comedian downstage alone — Booth's brain grasped the cue as though it were a trigger.

Quitting the theater, he spent the rest of midday darting here and there across town, lining up saddle horses, hobnobbing, conferring behind doors with his henchmen. The picture of fashion, he repaired to Mrs. Surratt's house about 4:00 P.M. Wiechmann, enjoying a Good Friday government holiday, was there. Then, departing on an errand, he caught a glimpse of Booth in the parlor, chatting with Mrs. Surratt.

When Wiechmann returned with a horse and buggy rented for a drive with the Widow Surratt to Surrattsville, Booth had gone. Mary

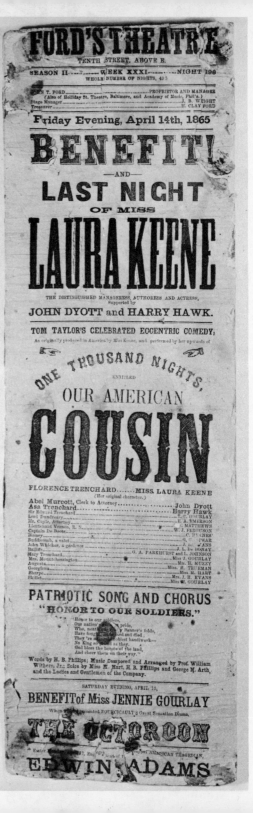

Ford's Theater program for the evening of April 14, 1865. It was picked up in Lincoln's box and is supposedly stained with his blood. (National Archives)

The Kirkwood Hotel where Booth left his calling card for Vice-President Andrew Johnson. (National Archives)

Surratt showed Wiechmann a small parcel — "a glass" that she said the actor had given her to take to Lloyd at the Surrattsville tavern.

Booth meanwhile had hurried to the nearby Herndon House to call on "Mr. Kincheloe." No one knows the words exchanged in the privacy of Lewis Paine's room. At any rate, Booth assigned to Paine a one-eyed roan horse and the mission of killing either General Grant or Secretary of State Seward.

From the Herndon House, Booth went to the Kirkwood Hotel. At the lobby desk he inquired for Atzerodt. He was not in. Upon this, John Wilkes Booth made a move as mystifying as any in a sorcerer's repertory. He asked for none other than Andrew Johnson. Told the Vice-President was out, he requested a card of the desk clerk and scribbled a message to Johnson: *"Don't wish to disturb you. Are you at home?"* He asked the desk clerk to give the card to the Vice-President, who lived there.

[26]

Having performed this strange piece of business, John Wilkes Booth next went to Pumphrey's Livery for a favorite mare — a little bay horse he admired because she could "run like a cat." A friend who saw him trotting her down the avenue later testified that Booth was "sitting like a Centaur. He was faultlessly dressed, [wearing] elegant riding boots with slender steel spurs. . . ."

Dozens of theater fans and acquaintances noticed Booth on the street that afternoon and he deliberately courted the attention of all. John Matthews, a stock company player, said he encountered Booth near Willard's Hotel. According to Matthews, Booth gave him a sealed letter to deliver next day to the editor of the *National Intelligencer*. Just then a company of Union troops marched past with a column of tattered Confederate prisoners. Booth blurted, "Great God! I no longer have a country!" and promptly rushed away.

Another person who encountered Booth that afternoon was Thomas B. Florence, editor of the *Daily Constitutional Union*. In his Saturday edition, Florence would report: ". . . in a short conversation he [Booth] stated . . . that he had lost about $6,000 in oil by the recent floods at Oil City. He appeared perfectly sober, though at times . . . abstracted. . . ."

A curtain fell on Booth's activities as the afternoon advanced into Good Friday evening. He met his accomplices somewhere and armed Paine and Atzerodt with revolvers, and (as later told by Atzerodt) assigned revised targets — Paine and Herold were to slay the Secretary of State; Atzerodt was to interecept and kill Vice-President Andrew Johnson. Probably these measures were designed as diversions to take attention away from the killing of the President.

At 9:30 P.M. Booth dismounted at the stage door of Ford's in "Baptist Alley." A Negress who lived in the alley heard the stage star shout, "Spangler!" The stagehand came out and so did a helper, a man known as "Peanut John" Burroughs. "Peanut John" held Booth's horse; the carpenter went back inside; Booth took a side passage around to the Tenth Street front of the playhouse.

Dropping into Taltavul's Saloon alongside the theater, Booth ordered brandy. Someone at the bar advised him he couldn't hold a candle to his father's acting. Booth stalked out in a fury. Over his shoulder he boasted that when he left the stage he'd be the most famous man in America.

Then John Wilkes braced himself and entered Ford's Theater with an offhand quip for doorkeeper Joseph Buckingham.

The play was in progress. With a black slouch hat in hand, Booth mounted the stairs to the dress circle. Numerous people in the audience noticed him as he threaded the side aisle heading toward the State Box. He made no effort to hide his matinee-idol profile. An Army officer seated on the aisle thought he saw Booth hand a card to an attendant at the outer door to the box. If so, who was this attendant, and why did he fail to stop Booth's entering? Lincoln's messenger, Charles Forbes, had been there earlier. But Forbes had left on an errand; his replacement was never identified.

It could only have been John Parker, a constable supposed to guard the box door throughout the evening. Parker then deserted his post. For no one challenged John Wilkes Booth, much less prevented him from entering the State Box. Conceivably Booth handed his name card, and an appropriate message or fee, to the invidious Parker, who then disappeared.

Stepping into the dim inner corridor, Booth quickly closed the door behind him, wedging it shut with a wooden upright from a music stand — an item Spangler or someone else had placed at hand for the purpose. Then Booth turned toward an inner door that gave onto the box and put his eye to a recently bored peephole. This offered a perfect bead on the exposed back of Lincoln's head. With an overcoat draped over his shoulders, the President sat in a high-backed rocker, his left elbow resting on the box rail. Squinting, Booth could discern Mrs. Lincoln at the President's right. An officer in evening dress, Major Henry R. Rathbone, and his fiancée, Miss Clara Harris, occupied a settee beyond. Booth could hear snatches of the comedy dialogue. His cue approached . . . — *"sockdolo-gizing old mantrap!"*

The house roared its laughter at the familiar line.

Booth opened the door, drew a derringer, and stepped into the box.

[28]

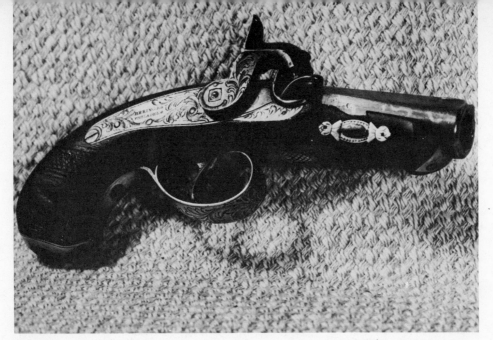

Booth's pistol, the gun that killed Abraham Lincoln. (National Park Service)

The derringer blazed and there was a hammerlike thud. Abraham Lincoln, slumping slightly, lowered his chin to his chest as though he had abruptly fallen asleep.

Major Rathbone reared on the settee, startled by the thud. He glimpsed a drift of smoke across the President's shoulder. Catching sight of Booth, Rathbone sprang. Booth dropped the gun and struck at him with a dagger, cutting the major's forearm to the bone. Unarmed and now sorely wounded, Rathbone made a valiant lunge at the wild-eyed intruder. Thrown to the balustrade of the box, Booth managed to get a leg over the rail and made a crazy jump for the stage some twelve feet below.

This acrobatic stunt was to prove the actor's undoing. Normally such a leap would have been a mere gymnastic exercise to the athletic Booth. Now, thrown off balance, he caught the spur of his left boot in a Treasury Guard flag that was draped about the box rail. The flag ripped.

Booth fell onto the stage, twisting his left leg under him as he did so and snapping the fibula above the ankle.

Someone screamed — it may have been Mrs. Lincoln — *"The President has been shot!"* Rathbone's fiancée, Clara Harris, cried out for help.

Lurching across the stage in a staggering run, Booth shouted something that sounded like *"Sic semper tyrannis!"* ("Ever thus to tyrants!") — the motto of Virginia. Harry Hawk, the lone actor on stage, thought the assassin shouted, "I've done it!" Booth struck at Laura Keene as he rushed past her in the wings. Backstage Booth slashed again at orchestra leader William Withers, Jr., and sent him reeling. "I recognized him as J. Wilkes Booth," Withers later testified, "and watched him make his exit into the alley."

Hatless, Booth plunged through the stage door brandishing the bloodstained dagger. Outside, little "Peanut John" waited with the bay mare. Booth knocked him down, kicked him aside. The momentum of his fury carried the crippled assassin in a single leap into the saddle. He roweled the mare's flank, and she tore down the alley toward the open street, just as a Washington attorney who had been in the audience bounded from the stage door in pursuit, crying, "Stop that man!" Conflicting versions muddled later reports, but according to Attorney Stewart, Booth raced from "Baptist Alley" into F Street. Then, like a black wind in the night, he was gone.

Back in the theater a riot had exploded. People fought in the aisles. Trampled children shrieked. There were maniacal cries of "Burn the playhouse!" and "Lynch the actors!" Naming the recognized assassin, men shouted, "Booth! That was Booth!" The *Cousin* cast was appalled. Helen Trueman, who played the ingenue role of Augusta, years later vividly recalled the nightmarish tumult. "Mrs. Lincoln's scream turned the house into an inferno. There will never be anything like it on earth. The shouts, groans, curses, smashing of seats, screams of women . . . created a pandemonium that . . . through all the ages will stand out as a hell of hells."

[30]

A young Army surgeon, Dr. Charles Leale, struggled to the door of Lincoln's box. Major Rathbone, dazed and bloody, dislodged the wedge to admit him. Another Army surgeon, Dr. Charles Taft, was hoisted into the box. Dr. A. F. A. King volunteered professional aid. Finding Lincoln "pulseless and apnoeic," Dr. Leale placed him on the floor and applied mouth-to-mouth respiration and diaphragm, closed-chest cardiac massage. This artificial respiration evoked a faint pulse.

A witness from the audience, William T. Kent, had aided Dr. Leale in cutting open Lincoln's clothing. At least a dozen other persons pressed forward to assist the doctors or attend Rathbone, Mrs. Lincoln, and hysterical Clara Harris. Laura Keene would recall taking the President's head in her lap. A fellow player, W. J. Ferguson, said anguished Laura merely stood by, looking on. But Ferguson's reporting could err. He described the President's wound as "a little dark spot no larger than the head of a lead pencil just under the right ear." Actually Booth's shot struck Lincoln behind the left ear.

Dr. Leale remarked "profound shock" and "great prostration." Evidence of brain damage at once convinced him the wound was mortal. The surgeons, consulting, decided death would be hastened by moving the stricken President to the White House. As troops now stormed in to clear the theater, it was decided to take Lincoln to a house across the street.

So they carried the unconscious President to the Petersen house opposite the theater. There he was placed on a bed in a small room at the rear of a ground-floor hall. The President's great frame had to be positioned diagonally to fit into the bed.

Probing with a finger, Dr. Taft could not locate the bullet. A 6-inch silver probe was sent for. This, too, proved unavailing. Everyone could see that the President was dying. His left upper eyelid was swollen, discolored from effused blood; the right eye, dilated and sightless, grew bloodshot and protuberant. Surgeon General Barnes was summoned.

The elusive ball lodged in Lincoln's brain was a brutal killer — a .44-caliber, handmade slug roughly half an inch in diameter. Made of

The Petersen house, across the street from Ford's Theater, where Abraham Lincoln died. An original Handy photograph.

so-called Britannia metal, this bullet was only a little harder than lead, and striking with sledgehammer force it could act like a rotating dumdum. Paper wadding and gunpowder had also been fired with great force into Lincoln's head. Surgeon General Barnes, working a rubber Nélaton probe, found the bullet at last. It was buried 7½ inches deep, directly behind Lincoln's right eye. Subsequent autopsy revealed a 1-inch disc of bone driven 3 inches into the brain, and a jagged splinter from the bullet deeper in. Most modern authorities agree that even today's neurosurgery (plasma, transfusions, and aseptic techniques included) could not have conquered this frightful wound. The marvel is that Lincoln thus stricken lived nine more hours.

[32]

And he survived those hours in an airless little bedroom crammed with sweaty soldiers, doctors, weeping mourners, horsemen, messengers — noisy with the hectic voices of excitement and hysteria. War Secretary Stanton soon arrived, and most of the cabinet followed. Mrs. Lincoln, their eldest son, Robert, and Lincoln's secretary, John Hay, were at the bedside periodically. Senators, politicians, officers, and clergymen crowded in for the deathwatch. Above the bed a halitosic gaslight flickered, and the smell of muddy boots and damp wool might have emanated from the picture over the bed — a commonplace reproduction of Rosa Bonheur's *Horse Fair*.

About 6:00 in the morning it began to drizzle. By 7:00 A.M. of that dark Saturday, the crowd in front of the Petersen house was drenched by a sifting rain.

Secretary of the Navy Gideon Welles remarked that the stifling atmosphere in the back room was unbearable.

Lincoln died at 7:22 in the morning of April 15, 1865.

Someone credited Stanton with voicing the memorable curtain line: "Now he belongs to the ages."

In Cold Blood—Mayhem Strikes Secretary Seward

David Herold, Booth's devoted vassal, spent a busy Good Friday in Washington on undercover activities. He stopped in at a room Atzerodt had taken at the Kirkwood. He visited Booth at the National Hotel. At Naylor's Livery he rented a roan mare. What he then did that afternoon has remained a mystery that defies investigation. Herold's ability to dodge daylight observation and erase his tracks certainly belied the character given him by family friends who described him as a "callow boy," or a simpleton.

William H. Seward, Secretary of State in Lincoln's Cabinet. On the conspirators'
murder list, he barely escaped death at the hands of Lewis Paine. (Library of
Congress)

Early that evening he reported for a rendezvous with Booth, Paine,
and Atzerodt. Booth directed him to guide Lewis Paine to Secretary of
State Seward's residence on Lafayette Square. Big Lewis regarded Herold
with disdain; his nickname for him was "Blab." But the underground
made strange bedfellows. As a drugstore delivery boy Herold had a street
gamin's acquaintance of midtown Washington. And Paine, never able to
orient himself in a city after dark, needed an escort.

Only recently Seward had been severely injured by a carriage acci-
dent. Herold suggested that Paine pose as a messenger delivering medicine
from Dr. Verdi. Fox and lion, they set out on a murderous mission.

About ten minutes after ten that fatal Friday evening the two in-
vaders reined up at the curb in front of the Seward mansion. Paine dis-

mounted and tied his one-eyed horse to a tree. Herold proposed to stand by as lookout. A one-man assault force, the big trooper strode purposefully to Seward's door.

In a third-floor bedchamber Seward lay immobilized in bed, his right arm in a sling, his neck and chin fixed rigidly in a surgical collar. Under the crest of white hair, his beakish countenance was chalky. Dozing in a stupor of sedation, he was attended by Sergeant George Robinson, a hospital corps veteran. His daughter, Fanny Seward, sat at hand as temporary nurse.

Downstairs a bell jangled. Expecting a physician, the Seward's butler, William Bell, answered the door. In dressing gown and slippers, Frederick Seward went to the stair landing to meet the caller. As the elder Seward son later attested, "a tall, well-dressed man presented himself and, informing the servant that he brought a message from Doctor Verdi, was allowed in. . . ." The stranger mounted the stairs. He asked admission to Secretary Seward's room. Frederick told him the Secretary could have no visitors. "Suddenly the man sprang up [the staircase] and, having drawn a revolver, pulled the trigger."

Six lives were in dire jeopardy when Lewis Paine aimed a Colt point-blank at Frederick Seward. The weapon jammed and misfired, frustrating an otherwise inevitable household massacre. Infuriated, Paine leapt at Frederick Seward and struck with the gun barrel again and again. Under this berserk attack, Frederick crumpled to the floor.

Paine hurled the broken Colt at his victim's bleeding head; then he snatched a Bowie knife from his belt and charged toward Secretary Seward's room. Bursting through the door, he hurled himself at the prostrate convalescent. Seward, dazed, somehow dodged the striking knife. Again and again Paine's homicidal blade flashed in the lamplight. His cheek sliced open, the stricken secretary of state cried out and tried to roll from the bed. Paine caught him by the hair and wrenched his head around, attempting to expose his throat. Twice the Bowie knife slashed under Seward's chin. Only the surgical collar — a metal brace to support a broken jaw — saved Seward from decapitation.

[35]

In frenzy, Paine tried to stab his victim's body. Jumbled bedding probably protected Seward as he slid from mattress to carpet. Now Paine was grabbed by hands from behind. Sergeant Robinson, rousing from shock, threw himself upon the killer as young Augustus Seward, summoned by Fanny's screams, dashed into the bedroom. There ensued a ferocious battle with Paine fighting like a carnivore. He stabbed Robinson, whirled, and almost scalped Augustus with a lightning slash. Tumbling furniture from his path, he roared out into the hall. A State Department messenger, Emerick Hansell, had started up the stairway. Squalling, "I'm mad! I'm mad!" Paine flung himself down the stairs. He daggered Hansell against the banister and reached the street door with a bound. Behind him he left five hideously injured victims sprawled in a welter of blood.

At the curb Paine stalled, glaring. The street was empty — "Blab" Herold had deserted him.

In the house behind him a window was thrown open; someone screamed, *"Murder! Murder!"*

His face streaming blood, Augustus Seward appeared in the lighted doorway, shouting.

In that moment Lewis Paine displayed a cool self-possession, a Spartan discipline, that surely precluded any possible defense of his conduct as insane. Alarmed he certainly must have been to find himself abandoned in this unfamiliar section of an enemy capital. But now, although gory as a gladiator, the deadly raider calmly untied his horse, swung into the saddle, and rode the animal at a walk up the street.

William Bell raced from the Seward house and ran after Paine, shrieking. Paine merely increased his roan's pace to a leisurely trot.

Shadowy figures who were starting to run across the square paid the cantering horseman no attention. No murderer would beat so casual a retreat from the scene of the crime.

But this one did. Even as John Wilkes Booth disappeared behind Ford's Theater, the savage Lewis Paine vanished in night-enshrouded Washington.

Riders in the Night—
The Assassins Escape

After he raced out of "Baptist Alley," Booth headed eastward for the Navy Yard Bridge that spanned the Anacostia River about two miles distant. The night was gusty, with green-gray clouds scudding across a yellow moon. Somewhere out on F Street, Booth headed toward Capitol Hill. The streets beyond the Capitol were pitch-dark except for an occasional lamp; good people were abed at this hour. No one hailed the lone rider. No one stopped him.

As a wartime precaution, the gate at the Washington end of the Navy Yard Bridge had been ordered closed to travelers at 9:00 P.M. True, this order had recently been rescinded, but the bridge guard had nevertheless been warned to remain on the alert. On this fatal Friday night the guard happened to be under the command of Sergeant Silas T. Cobb.

About 10:45 that evening, Cobb heard fast hoofbeats coming through the night. He roused his sentries and positioned himself at the bridge gate to intercept the horseman racing out of Eleventh Street. A lathered bay mare reared up. As Cobb later testified, the hatless rider was otherwise clad like a "gentleman," from stock to elegant black boots. His face seemed pale in striking contrast to his glossy black mustache.

Challenged and questioned, the rider gave the name of Booth. He said he was going home from the District; that he lived downcountry near Beantown, Maryland; that he'd waited until after nine o'clock to cross the bridge because the early evening had been dark and he wanted moonlight for the journey. Satisfied, Sergeant Cobb waved the horseman to go ahead. Not long after that, a second rider galloped out of the night mist. This was an unprepossessing younger man. Disliking his looks, Cobb caught the newcomer's bridle and brought him under a bridgehead lamp for questioning.

The old Navy Yard Bridge across the Potomac River where Booth escaped from Washington. (National Archives)

The young man said his name was "Smith." At Cobb's snort of disbelief, he changed it to "Thomas." He said he was bound southward to White Plains, his home. Why at this late hour? The young man, leering, said he had "been with a woman." To the soldier there seemed nothing unusual about this. He gave the nod, and the youth, later identified as David Herold, trotted across the Navy Yard Bridge to the southbound open road.

Somewhere below Anacostia the fugitive pair joined company at a doubtless prearranged rendezvous. Side by side, they rode on in the night — a warped and vicious Don Quixote and a slavish, doting Sancho Panza. One can imagine them exchanging experiences — Booth's theatrical boasts, Herold's glib and flippant recital. No one would ever know how the latter justified his abandonment of Lewis Paine; case analysts have since wondered whether Booth had secretly planned to "sacrifice" the hulking brute — a technique common to underground practice. Obviously Booth went along with Paine's being "dumped"; the actor preferred the sly Herold for a backcountry guide.

Booth rode in pain on the eleven-mile gallop to Surrattsville. His fractured shin had begun to swell. When they pulled up at the tavern Mary Surratt had leased to alcoholic John Lloyd, Booth was groaning in agony.

They ordered Lloyd to fetch weapons, field glass, and saddle gear previously cached in the tavern. (Afterward the bleary-eyed innkeeper swore he had no inkling as to why the guns were wanted.)

Booth gulped some whiskey, then inquired for the nearest doctor. It appeared the local physician was no longer in practice. The fugitive riders spurred off, leaving Lloyd staring after them.

About 2:00 A.M. on April 15 they posted through the hamlet named "T.B." Here Booth and Herold veered from the T.B.–Piscataway–Port Tobacco road and headed westward on a back road toward Bryantown. They were seeking the help of a Dr. Samuel Mudd and a haven where they could hide. For soon they would be in need of sanctuary.

And pursuit should have come sooner than later. For that fateful Friday night, a third rider had galloped out of the Eleventh Street gloom at the head of Navy Yard Bridge. This horseman reached the bridge about 11:00 P.M. He asked Sergeant Cobb if an unkempt youth on a roan had recently crossed over. When Cobb said yes, this third rider declared himself to be John Fletcher, foreman at Naylor's Livery in Washington. He said he was after a stolen roan, probably the same one this youth was riding. Having spotted the animal in midtown Washington and given chase, he figured the suspect planned to sell the rented horse in Lower Maryland — a common practice in those times. Fletcher asked Cobb to let him cross the bridge and overtake the roan.

Sergeant Cobb demurred. The hour was late; if Fletcher crossed over now, he wouldn't be allowed to return until tomorrow morning. Muttering in wrath, stable foreman Fletcher wheeled his mount and headed back toward the darkened Capitol.

Of course, the bridge guard at this hour had no way of knowing about the President's assassination that night in midtown Washington. But had the alarm immediately been rushed to this important bridge on Washington's southerly perimeter, Cobb would perforce have reported Booth's crossing and Herold's, and cavalry might easily have overtaken Lincoln's assassins. As it was, no alarm went to Navy Yard Bridge that night. By sheer luck, it was stableman Fletcher who provided the authorities with the first clue as to the getaway route taken by the fugitive assassins. . . .

America's Biggest Manhunt—A Dragnet with Many Holes

In the wake of the assassination, three law enforcement organizations went into haphazard action. First in the field was Washington's Metropolitan Police Force under Superintendent A. C. Richards; then the Army's Military Police with provost marshals under General C. C. Augur, District of Columbia commandant; finally and belatedly, the Federal Secret Service under General Lafayette Baker. All three came under a military dictatorship exercised by War Secretary Stanton — an assumption of supreme authority that left some strange question marks over the manhunt operation. At the outset, service rivalries and status jealousies clogged the emergency machinery.

This was no fault of Police Superintendent Richards — an officer who coupled competence with initiative and drive. By chance he had been a spectator in Ford's Theater that Good Friday night. He was among those who immediately recognized the assassin. At once Richards dashed to the lobby to ascertain the whereabouts of Constable John Parker, the policeman selected (against Richards' advice) to guard Lincoln's box.

The riot that swamped the playhouse drowned any chance of locating Parker. Richards rushed on down Tenth Street to Metropolitan Police headquarters, not far from Ford's. There, without a moment's delay, he mustered the city's detective force, dispatched patrols to scour the area for the assassin, and sped a messenger to Army headquarters on Madison Place (near Seward's residence) to alert the military police.

By 11:30 P.M. Richards' detectives were nosing around the National Hotel; scouting the Surratt house at 541 H Street; questioning the cast at Ford's, and taking depositions of one witness after another who named Booth the assassin. Also on the blotter Richards had the name of John Surratt and a description of Lewis Paine.

Then in came stableman Fletcher to report chasing a horse thief to Navy Yard Bridge. Fletcher was sent to Army headquarters to tell his tale to General C. C. Augur. With seventeen witness depositions on record, by midnight Major Richards was certain of Lincoln's killer, and he was also sure of the road the fugitive assassins had taken. Eager to dispatch a flying squad down the trail into Lower Maryland, he appealed to Augur's headquarters, requesting horses for a police posse.

Had General Augur provided the desired mounts, Richards' constabulary might have overtaken Booth before morning. But Augur answered Richards with a negative. It seemed the Army had no horses to spare. Historian O. H. Oldroyd would later attribute this to governmental "red tape." Modern historian Otto Eisenschiml observes, "the reasons for Augur's refusal are not apparent." General Augur in fact had herds of Army cavalry at disposal.

Major James R. O'Beirne, District Provost Marshal, proved to be another alert, efficient officer. Advised of the shooting at Ford's, he quickly checked John Wilkes Booth's address and dispatched Army detectives to the National Hotel. In Booth's room, detective Asahel Hitchcox found a jackpot in the actor's wardrobe trunk. Amongst garments (by one account including a Confederate colonel's uniform), photographs, and memento mori were a code acrostic, an indecipherable map; a letter from "Jenny" in Canada informing Booth she was sending a "rubber coat (or boat)," a letter from Booth's mother mentioning his engagement to a

[41]

```
ZABCDEFGHIJKLMNOPQRSTUVWXYZ
ABCDEFGHIJKLMNOPQRSTUVWXYZA
BCDEFGHIJKLMNOPQRSTUVWXYZAB
CDEFGHIJKLMNOPQRSTUVWXYZABC
DEFGHIJKLMNOPQRSTUVWXYZABCD
EFGHIJKLMNOPQRSTUVWXYZABCDE
FGHIJKLMNOPQRSTUVWXYZABCDEF
GHIJKLMNOPQRSTUVWXYZABCDEFG
HIJKLMNOPQRSTUVWXYZABCDEFGH
IJKLMNOPQRSTUVWXYZABCDEFGHI
JKLMNOPQRSTUVWXYZABCDEFGHIJ
KLMNOPQRSTUVWXYZABCDEFGHIJK
LMNOPQRSTUVWXYZABCDEFGHIJKL
MNOPQRSTUVWXYZABCDEFGHIJKLM
NOPQRSTUVWXYZABCDEFGHIJKLMN
OPQRSTUVWXYZABCDEFGHIJKLMNO
PQRSTUVWXYZABCDEFGHIJKLMNOP
QRSTUVWXYZABCDEFGHIJKLMNOPQ
RSTUVWXYZABCDEFGHIJKLMNOPQR
STUVWXYZABCDEFGHIJKLMNOPQRS
TUVWXYZABCDEFGHIJKLMNOPQRSTU
UVWXYZABCDEFGHIJKLMNOPQRSTU
VWXYZABCDEFGHIJKLMNOPQRSTUV
WXYZABCDEFGHIJKLMNOPQRSTUVW
XYZABCDEFGHIJKLMNOPQRSTUVWX
YZABCDEFGHIJKLMNOPQRSTUVWXY
ZABCDEFGHIJKLMNOPQRSTUVWXYZ
```

*The secret-code acrostic found in Booth's trunk.
(National Archives)*

"young lady in Washington society," and a missive implicating one Samuel Arnold of Baltimore in the assassination conspiracy. This note advised Booth: *"Do not act rashly or in haste."* And it urged: *"Go and see how it will be taken at R——d, and ere long I shall be better prepared to again be with you."*

O'Beirne passed these items to a Lieutenant Tyrrell (or Terry) for assessment. The collection presently grew with specimens garnered by special detective John Lee, dispatched by O'Beirne as a bodyguard for Andrew Johnson at the Kirkwood House. A canny professional, Lee dug up pay dirt. The Vice-President wasn't there that midnight. But Lee, combing the bar, learned Booth had been in, asking for a grubby houseguest named Atzerodt. Lee procured the hotel passkey, went to the German's room and walked into a virtual crime museum.

On an inside hook a coat dangled. In it Lee found a Canadian bankbook inscribed "J. Wilkes Booth." A lump in the bed divulged a Colt revolver. Other finds included boxes of pistol ammunition, a Bowie knife,

[42]

a handkerchief monogrammed "Mary R. E. Booth," a pair of new gauntlets, a brass spur. Lee rushed these items to O'Beirne, and George A. Atzerodt went on the wanted list.

By that hour Booth's getaway companion was also identified. The key clue remains obscure, but soon after the assassination an ace detective named Rosch procured from a ledger in a midtown drugstore the signature of David E. Herold.

So far, so good; with the exception of General Augur's poor performance. Not only had he refused to mount a police posse; he failed to check Fletcher's story and question the guard at Navy Yard Bridge. Indeed, although Augur issued a general alarm at 11:45 P.M., with an order to arrest anyone attempting to leave the city, no couriers were dispatched to Washington's several bridgeheads with the order. Sergeant Cobb later testified he received no word of the assassination until breakfast time on Saturday. Apparently Augur was overwhelmed that night. With the District swept by riot, excursion, and alarm, he deferred to the command decisions of War Secretary Stanton.

In a side room at the Petersen house, Edwin M. Stanton seized the reins of supreme command. In a frenzy of excitement he issued a spate of orders, sent messengers helter-skelter, summoned adjutants and cabinet members, bellowed at subalterns, and dictated rapid-fire memoranda to Corporal James Tanner, a shorthand expert fortuitously at the scene. All night long Stanton juggled War Department directives, military moves, statecraft, civil defense, and police detail on the one hand, while interrogating witnesses and conducting a drumhead police inquest on the other.

It was an astonishing performance, a show of emergency leadership unparalleled in American history. Stanton even went so far as to pronounce Washington in a state of siege — a decree that mobilized all military forces in the District of Columbia and sent artillery crews racing to man the guns of the outlying forts. He telegraphed the New York police chief, requesting him to send that city's foremost detectives. He called for Navy monitors and gunboats to prepare for action in the Lower Potomac and Chesapeake Bay. He wired the head of the B.&O. Railroad to stop

[43]

Grant's northbound train and return the general to Washington under heavy military escort. He posted infantry around his residence and the homes of cabinet colleagues; sent General Sherman a warning to guard against assassins; and seized Ford's Theater, ordering the blanket arrest of the management, stage crew, and entire cast of *Our American Cousin*.

In consequence, Washington spun in a pyrotechnic pinwheel of turmoil. Much misdirected effort went to arm the city's defenses against all-out attack. Riot and panic caused a diversion of police, as well as military, detail. Grilling witnesses, Stanton merely duplicated most of the investigation conducted by Superintendent Richards. And some of Stanton's dictates and decrees were legally insupportable. Surely the arrest of the players at Ford's was unjust to Laura Keene, Hawk, and other innocent bystanders of the cast.

And Stanton, too, failed to order the District bridges immediately closed. At 11:30 P.M. he telegraphed a cavalry station north of Washington: "THE ASSASSINS ARE SUPPOSED TO HAVE ESCAPED TOWARD MARYLAND." Since Maryland flanked the District on three sides, a fuzzier dispatch could hardly be imagined.

Stranger still was Stanton's failure to dispatch an immediate alarm identifying Booth as the wanted murderer. According to Corporal Tanner, shortly after midnight he had "testimony enough to hang Booth . . . higher than Haman." At 2:10 A.M., Saturday, April 15, Stanton's first official press release left the assassin still anonymous.

Shortly after midnight, Stanton had held a top secret conference at the Petersen house. Charles Dana, Assistant Secretary of War, attended. So did General Augur and Provost Marshal O'Beirne. Police Superintendent Richards sat in. Chief Justice Cartter and a detective captain who knew Booth also attended. At this conference, Stanton said he was satisfied John Wilkes Booth was the assassin, but he wanted to delay making this public. The war chief gave his subordinates no reason for this. However, during the conference Stanton must have heard from Richards concerning the horsemen who crossed Navy Yard Bridge. If so, there was no reaction. And not until 3:20 A.M., five hours after the assassination, was J. Wilkes

Booth named in an official press release. By that hour, the dispatch was too late for the morning editions.

But it was the failure to block the road to Surrattsville and Port Tobacco that has remained a puzzle to history. With the B.&O. Railroad under interdict, a virtual naval blockade guarding the Chesapeake and Lower Potomac, regiments of infantry and cavalry blocking all highways north, east, and west, and Long Bridge (to Alexandria, Virginia), and the Chain Bridge (to Fairfax) and Benning Bridge (due east) closed to traffic, the Navy Yard Bridge over the Anacostia and the back road south to Richmond still remained wide open. Not the least baffling element of this puzzle was contributed years afterward by one of the bridge sentries, F. A. Demond of Cavendish, Vermont, who swore in a deposition that both Booth and Herold uttered the secret Army countersign, "T. B. Road," thus gaining Sergeant Cobb's permission to pass. Although the sergeant never mentioned this countersign, his testimony revealed other gaps, and the escapers may indeed have been provided with the key password. Be that as it was, the Navy Yard Bridge remained an open door. And not until 4:00 A.M. Saturday did the Army chief send Federal cavalry down the trail into Lower Maryland. By that time Booth and his companion had had a six-hour start on the Federal pursuit. . . .

In the dark before dawn of that Easter Saturday, Booth and Herold reached the isolated homestead of Dr. Samuel Mudd. Later the doctor testified that Herold, knocking at the door, called out that a rider, "Mr. Tyson," had been hurt by a fall and needed medical attention. If Dr. Mudd, as he afterward declared, failed to recognize Booth in the outer darkness, he must have acted with a disregard of danger for himself and his wife in readily admitting at that hour two disheveled, whiskey-scented travelers, both bearing side arms. Apparently he did not arm himself before opening the door, nor bother to summon the handyman on the place.

According to Dr. Mudd, Booth kept his face hidden, chin lowered, a shawl pulled up — surely a suspicious mien. However, Dr. Mudd aided

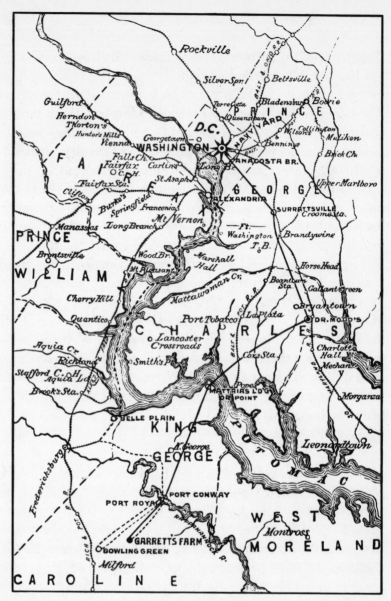

Map showing the routes of Booth and the detectives, and the place where Booth was shot and Herold captured. The solid line represents Booth's route and the broken line that of Herold's.

Dr. Samuel Mudd, the country physician who set Booth's broken leg. (Library of Congress)

the injured man in hopping to a parlor sofa. He cut the boot from Booth's swollen foot, set the bone, and applied a makeshift splint. Mrs. Mudd brought food and hot coffee. Herold (he introduced himself as "Henson") helped the doctor carry Booth to an upstairs bedroom.

Herold then drifted out, presumably to sleep in the barn. At noontime Dr. Mudd reexamined the injured man's leg while Booth kept his face turned aside. Mudd said that he asked no questions of this peculiar patient. Without ado he furnished Booth with a crude pair of homemade crutches. He let Booth nap throughout that afternoon. At twilight, while the doctor was gone from the house on an errand, the crippled man and his companion departed.

It would seem Dr. Mudd breathed a sigh of relief at this departure — he had not liked the language Herold used in front of Mrs. Mudd. If this kindly physician observed a "good riddance," his mistrust was unquestionably belated. For Dr. Mudd was going to pay a grueling price for harboring these two fugitives.

[47]

Deriding Mudd's defenders who contended that he was simply a humane country doctor doing his duty, the Federal government would actually pronounce him an assassination accomplice who abetted Booth's escape. And it appears Dr. Mudd did tell Booth and Herold of a backwoods shortcut to the home of Colonel Samuel Cox whose Wicomico-Potomac plantation had served as a way station and spy haven on the Confederate underground.

Following the southbound trail to Cox's that Saturday night, Booth and Herold became lost in the interior of dismal Zekiah Swamp. Booth suffered much on horseback. He suffered more in trying to plod through the mire on his crutches. It was some time after midnight when the exhausted pair reached Cox's Farm. There they learned that no boat was immediately available for the Potomac crossing and that Federal horsemen and "Blue-bellies" were now in the area "thicker than fiddlers in hell."

Booth and Herold took cover. Colonel Cox's foster brother Thomas A. Jones, a former Rebel undergrounder, led them to a hideout in nearby woods on the Cox plantation. For the next six days and five nights Cox and Jones would shelter and feed the desperate escapees.

One of the question marks that lingers over the Booth manhunt concerns this stay at Cox's. For Stanton and his War Department minions subsequently "threw the book" at Dr. Mudd, who had harbored Booth for only a few hours and at a time when Booth's name had not been broadcast. Indeed, upon learning of Lincoln's assassination from a neighbor, Dr. Mudd went to his Unionist brother, George Mudd, and told him to advise the Federals that suspicious characters had been at the house. Thus Dr. Mudd brought military vengeance down on his own head. But these same Federal authorities were to completely hush up and ultimately forget about Booth's six-day sojourn with the subversive Colonel Cox. . . .

In Washington, Major Richards must have been puzzled by the silence Stanton initially imposed on Booth's name. Still, for his own satisfaction, the Metropolitan Police superintendent had other fish to fry. His detectives had found linked to the names of Booth and Herold the name of John Surratt. Fast sleuthing led to the boardinghouse at 541 H Street. At 2:00 A.M., Easter Saturday, Richards ordered the place raided on the chance that Booth had dodged into hiding there. When detective John Clarvoe and his squad rang Mrs. Surratt's bell, they roused star boarder Louis Wiechmann.

He expressed horror and astonishment when told Lincoln had been assassinated. So did Mrs. Surratt when she emerged from her bedroom. The widow, accompanied by Wiechmann, had that afternoon driven to Surrattsville, to discuss a real estate loan (she said) owed a Mr. Nothey. Returning to Washington at suppertime, they had watched early fireworks and heard echoing band music — manifests of a victory celebration that led Mrs. Surratt (as Wiechmann recalled it) to utter something baleful about wicked people and the wages of sin. Now, informed of Lincoln's death, she voiced a shocked exclamation.

Questioned by Clarvoe, she admitted John Wilkes Booth had called at the boardinghouse around two o'clock the previous afternoon, asking for her son. But John Surratt was not in the city. Where was he? She couldn't say. She declared she had not seen him for the past two weeks. Wiechmann gave this an affirmative nod, and volunteered to call at police headquarters at 8:00 A.M. to aid the constables any way he could. Somewhat disarmed, Clarvoe and his squad withdrew — but to a vantage point where they could keep Mrs. Surratt's domicile under surveillance.

Coincident with this early-morning episode, Captain D. H. L. Gleason put in a breathless appearance at Augur's headquarters. "I told them," he testified later, ". . . all I knew about the persons suspected, and I . . . also asked for a cavalry squad to go with me to the Surratt place in Maryland, as I thought the assassin would escape that way." Gleason met with a response similar to the one that stymied Police Superintendent Richards.

It was not until about 4:00 A.M. that Augur dispatched a small cavalry troop under Lieutenant David D. Dana, younger brother of the assistant war secretary, with orders to scout down through Lower Maryland. Dana went to Piscataway. There at 7:00 A.M. he rushed a rider on down to

[49]

Chapel Hill to alert this Potomac cavalry post and spread a "description of the parties who committed the deed." Dana's descriptive broadcasts must have been wanting in accuracy. In a 7:00 A.M. report to Washington, he stated he had "reliable" information that Seward's assailant was a criminal highwayman named "Boyce or Boyd."

From Piscataway, Lieutenant Dana led his troopers eastward to Bryantown, Maryland. There he pitched camp and sat down to await developments. Sheer luck had brought these Blue horsemen to a spot about four miles from the Mudd homestead, where Booth then lay in an exhausted stupor. But Dana's cavalry moved no closer.

In Washington, Police Superintendent Richards finally got mounted at 8:00 A.M. Riding with him, as a somewhat reluctant volunteer, was Louis Wiechmann. Like an arrow, Richards headed his constabulary for Surrattsville. But the squad did not arrive at the objective in good time. Augur had provided Richards with a batch of old nags literally ready for the boneyard. The poor beasts ended the eleven-mile run at a walk. Booth and Herold, of course, had long since gone.

Richards' detectives, ferreting around Surrattsville, did learn that the Booth crew had occasionally forgathered at Mrs. Surratt's tavern with John Surratt. From the bartender there they heard that on his last visit Surratt had said he intended to go on up to Montreal.

Richards led his squad on their blown horses back to Washington. He was not empty-handed. Back at Metropolitan headquarters he held Wiechmann incommunicado and sent for War Department permission to dispatch a detective team to New York City on a manhunt mission. The police superintendent did not specify the quarry nor mention Montreal. Evidently Richards mistrusted the Army high command, and, fearing he might again be hamstrung, determined to follow the trail on his own. Granted permission, he dispatched special officer James McDevitt with Wiechmann and John Holohan (another of Mrs. Surratt's boarders) to New York to hunt for John Surratt. War Department instructions limited their trip to that metropolis and ordered a prompt return to Washington to "report to these [Stanton's] headquarters." On his own initiative Richards extended the mission to Canada.

Meanwhile, Stanton had other manhunt plans. Shortly before Saturday noon on April 15 the war secretary dispatched a telegram to Brigadier General Lafayette Baker, Astor House, New York City: COME HERE IMMEDIATELY AND SEE IF YOU CAN FIND THE MURDERER OF THE PRESIDENT.

Thus America's self-styled master manhunter, the chief of the Federal Secret Service, belatedly entered the game.

Conspiracy Roundup—Catch as Catch Can

Baker received Stanton's summoning telegram at 3:00 P.M. on Saturday, April 15. He could not reach Washington until Easter Sunday morning.

Nothing in the record, then, seems more unaccountable than the reception Baker got from the Secretary of War. According to the Secret Service chief, Augur's military headquarters snubbed him icily and gave him no information on the manhunt. He sought out the war secretary to get it from the horse's mouth. Emotionally Stanton confided that the enemy *"have now performed what they long threatened to do; they have killed the President."* And he told Baker, *"You must go to work; my whole dependence is upon you."* But when Baker asked about current manhunt details Stanton advised him, *"No direct clue has been obtained beyond the simple conceded fact that J. Wilkes Booth was the assassin."*

Nothing about the conspiratorial evidence found in Booth's trunk. Nor the items discovered at the Kirkwood House. Nor testimony pointing to Navy Yard Bridge, Surrattsville, and a certain boardinghouse on H Street. Why did the war secretary withhold vital detail from the very officer he placed in charge of the manhunt? General Baker's word on this might be suspect because his word on anything was. Yet months later Colonel H. L. Burnett of the judge advocate's office wrote: *"while it was rumored and generally believed that Booth was the assassin, for some days this rested only upon the statements of some of the persons at the theater."*

With the National Hotel and Kirkwood House findings seemingly too top secret for anyone except Augur and Secretary Stanton, the manhunt had slowed to a standstill that Easter Sunday. Left on his own, Baker, with his ear to Pennsylvania Avenue, soon linked the names of Booth, Herold, and John Surratt. To his professional astonishment he learned that no photographs or descriptions of the fugitives had been published, although the Washington Common Council had voted $20,000 reward for their capture. "I immediately secured pictures of those mentioned . . . had them copied . . . and printed a circular." This flyer featured descriptions of the wanted assassins and offered an additional $10,000 reward for their apprehension.

Beginning Monday, April 17, Baker's agents papered the countryside with these posters. A photograph of John Wilkes Booth affixed to the broadside could be called a good likeness. But the Surratt picture was almost featureless, and Herold's a schoolboy portrait that bore little resemblance to the way he looked in 1865.

These early circulars contained no picture of Lewis Paine. Nor was he even named. But while the broadside offered only the sketchiest description of Booth, including such odd bits as "wears large seal ring on little finger, and when talking inclines his head forward; looks down," Baker's circular presented an almost photographic word portrait of Paine with such minutae as "wore double-breasted sack overcoat . . . new, heavy boots; voice small and thin inclined to tenor. . . ."

Baker must have procured this verbal portraiture from the Seward household — a sharp job of investigative reporting. While the Secret Service chief might be as unscrupulous as a Barbary pirate, he could exert genuine capability with a fat jackpot in prospect.

With $30,000 at stake Baker meant to let no grass grow. Unques-

$30,000 REWARD

DESCRIPTION

OF

JOHN WILKES BOOTH!

Who Assassinated the PRESIDENT on the Evening of April 14th, 1865.

Height 5 feet 8 inches; weight 160 pounds; compact built; hair jet black, inclined to curl. medium length. parted behind; eyes black, and heavy dark eye-brows; wears a large seal ring on little finger; when talking inclines his head forward; looks down.

Description of the Person who Attempted to Assassinate Hon. W. H. Seward, Secretary of State.

Height 6 feet 1 inch; hair black, thick, full and straight; no beard, nor appearance of beard; cheeks red on the jaws; face moderately full; 22 or 23 years of age; eyes. color not known—large eyes. not prominent; brows not heavy. but dark; face not large, but rather round; complexion healthy; nose straight and well formed, medium size; mouth small; lips thin; upper lip protruded when he talked; chin pointed and prominent; head medium size; neck short. and of medium length; hands soft and small; fingers tapering; shows no signs of hard labor; broad shoulders; taper waist; straight figure; strong looking man; manner not gentlemanly, but vulgar; Overcoat double-breasted. color mixed of pink and grey spots, small —was a sack overcoat, pockets in side and one on the breast, with lappells or flaps; pants black. common stuff; new heavy boots; voice small and thin, inclined to tenor.

The Common Council of Washington. D. C., have offered a reward of $20,000 for the arrest and conviction of these Assassins, in addition to which I will pay $10.000.

L. C. BAKER,
Colonel and Agent War Department.

Lafayette Baker's first reward poster issued after the assassination. Note the great detail on Seward's assailant, but the skimpy description of Booth. (Library of Congress)

SURRAT.   BOOTH.   HAROLD.

War Department, Washington, April 20, 1865,

$100,000 REWARD!

Stanton's reward poster issued six days after the murder. Note the unrecognizable pictures of Surratt and Herold and misspellings of their names. (Library of Congress)

tionably he took a dim view when General Augur's command suddenly came up with an unexpected haul. . . .

For Monday morning saw a catch of small fry — stagehand Ned Spangler; Michael O'Laughlin, Booth's friend from Baltimore; and Samuel Arnold, author of the "Sam" letter found in Booth's abandoned trunk.

Spangler was probably picked up on a tip from Jacob Ritterspaugh, a sceneshifter at Ford's. O'Laughlin, arrested in Baltimore, was probably reported by a local informer. He protested that his arrest "would be the death of my mother." His forecast proved accurate enough, except in one respect — his mother was not the one doomed.

Samuel Arnold was snared at Fortress Monroe, Virginia, where he had gone to work as a clerk. Baltimore Provost Marshal McPhail's officers also made this arrest. Later, War Department initiates would imply Arnold's capture resulted from discovery of the "Sam" letter. However, McPhail's Baltimore office did not know of the top-secret evidence uncovered by Augur's provosts in Washington, D.C. Probably Arnold, too, was turned in by an informer.

Then Augur's forces made a big catch. Early that Monday Provost Marshal O'Beirne dispatched a cavalry squadron under Army Lieutenant Alexander Lovett down into Lower Maryland. With Lovett rode Captain William Williams, an ace tracker.

Lovett's squadron galloped directly to Surrattsville — right to the door of Mrs. Surratt's crossroads tavern. Wasting no words, Lovett arrested tavern-keeper John M. Lloyd on a tip that must have come from one of Richards' constables.

With the muzzle of an Army revolver figuratively, if not literally, in his mouth, Lloyd talked his head off. What he said sent Lovett and his cavalrymen hightailing it down the pike to Bryantown. That evening Lovett conferred with young Lieutenant Dana at the Bryantown Hotel. Apparently Dana gave him a delayed report from George Mudd to the effect that two strange horsemen, one with a broken leg, had visited the house of Dr. Samuel Mudd the morning after Lincoln's assassination.

That was all Lieutenant Lovett needed. However, he decided he must first get some sleep. In so doing, he missed his chance at the $30,000 reward money.

For his part Captain Williams remained in Surrattsville long enough to sweat the miserable Lloyd. Thrown into an improvised guardhouse, the tavern-keeper blubbered a lengthy statement. The gist of it was that John Surratt had asked him to conceal some guns and other gear in the tavern, and that Mrs. Surratt came there the Tuesday before the assassination and told him they would be wanted soon. Lloyd said she had visited him again on Good Friday and told him "those things" would be called for that night. She had also asked Lloyd to have two bottles of whiskey ready for whoever came.

Lloyd's statement, subsequently sworn to, was to seal the doom of

Mary Eugenia Surratt. For on Monday night of the seventeenth, the man-hunters trapped big game.

Actually, Mary Surratt's approaching doom had its beginning early on Easter Sunday when a servant girl, Susan Jackson, informed a neighbor, J. H. Kimball, that the previous night three mysterious callers visited the Surratt house. Feigning sleep in her basement room, the girl overheard these men tell Mrs. Surratt that her son had been with Booth in Ford's Theater. On Monday Mr. Kimball reported this tale to the provost marshal general's office. At 11:00 P.M., General Augur ordered Colonel H. S. Olcott to dispatch a squad of special officers to arrest the widow and her household.

After posting pickets down the street, detectives Smith, Wermerskirch, and Morgan went up to Mrs. Surratt's door. Her daughter, Anna, answered the bellpull, and the three went in. Mrs. Surratt looked at them from down the hall. As decently as they could, they explained that she and her lodgers were wanted for questioning at military police headquarters. Would she arouse the guests and dress to go out?

Anna Surratt protested. But her mother finally expressed resignation. The detectives waited while the ladies went to summon the others and put on street attire. About 11:15 P.M. heavy footsteps sounded on the outside stoop and the bell jangled. Admitted by one of the plainclothesmen, a strapping young fellow shouldering a pickax stepped in. He wore mud-caked workman's clothes and a stocking cap made of a cut-off shirtsleeve pulled over his thick, dark hair. Scowling, he asked for Mrs. Surratt.

Questioned by officers Wermerskirch and Morgan, he muttered an incoherent name and said the widow had hired him to dig a garden. At this time of night? No, he'd come to see about tomorrow morning's work. Mrs. Surratt appeared on the scene. When she caught sight of the ditch-digger she recoiled in alarm. *"Before God I never saw that man before; I did not hire him; I don't know anything about him!"* Anna began to sob. She said the laborer with the pickax had come there to kill them.

At a signal, Olcott's other men came crowding into the house. The ladies were hustled out to a carriage. The detectives seized the intruder's pick and pinned him back against the wall. Officer Sampson identified the captive; it appeared he matched Colonel's Olcott's description of the invader who assaulted Secretary Seward.

The prisoner denied that he had ever been in the Confederate service. He said he had been in Washington only "six or eight days." Where had he slept on the night of Friday, April 14? He said he could not remember. Saturday night? He did not know. Easter Sunday night? He said, "In the depot." Under subsequent interrogation, he said he had spent the nights in question in a tree.

He was taken to Augur's headquarters. There the officers searched him from head to toe. In addition to twenty-five dollars in currency (money he could not explain) his muddy garments disgorged a litter of strange oddments. The inventory included an expensive compass, a bottle of hair grease, a toothbrush in a wooden case, a box of Colt pistol ammunition, a news clipping of Lincoln's inaugural address, a second toothbrush, a man's hairbrush, and a pocket dictionary — certainly a magpie clutter for the pockets of a day laborer. Significantly, however, the compass pointed directly to involvement with the Confederate underground. And the dictionary was a dead giveaway to officers acquainted with secret codes based on word transference and alphabetical substitution. In any case, the Colt ammunition jibed with the gun carried by Lewis Paine. Secretary Seward's houseboy was sent for. Without hesitation he identified the prisoner as the invader who ravaged the Seward residence.

So the guards clamped irons on Lewis Thornton Powell, alias Paine or Payne, alias Hull, Wood, Kincheloe. And he was locked up with Spangler, O'Laughlin, and Arnold in the iron hold of U.S. monitor *Saugus* at the Navy Yard.

Meanwhile, the Widow Surratt was being interrogated by one of Augur's best officers, Colonel John A. Foster. She had little chance in a question and answer match with an experienced lawyer. Foster held all the cards. Unknown to Mrs. Surratt, officer Rosch, combing her house from basement to attic, had come up with more evidence. This included a photo portrait of John Wilkes Booth, hidden in Anna's room, a bullet mold, and several letters that appeared to contain passages in code.

Mrs. Surratt admitted that her son knew Booth. She said Booth never discussed politics at her house. She insisted her son had gone to Canada. Asked if John Surratt had ever gone to Richmond, she declared, *"He has never been away long enough to go South and back."* Did she know the ditchdigger who came to her door? *"No, sir, the ruffian . . . he was a tremendous hard fellow. . . . I believe he would have murdered us. . . ."*

Mrs. Surratt's tongue stumbled painfully in this exchange. Obviously, in maternal anxiety, she tried to cover for her son in saying he had never been away long enough to "go South." Yet Wiechmann had already told the authorities about John's trip to Richmond with Mrs. Slater. And her statement about not recognizing Paine at her door was fatal. Years later Mrs. Surratt's apologists would try to present her as nearsighted. Perhaps she was. But the "Reverend Wood" had lodged at her house for a week. Surely she must have known his voice. And if she didn't recognize him, sharp-eyed Anna and a cousin were there at her side when Paine came to her house that night.

Directly after the interrogation by Foster, Mrs. Surratt and her daughter were confined in the Old Capitol Prison. . . .

Although the arrest of Mrs. Surratt and Lewis Paine were feathers in the Army's cap, as of Tuesday, April 18, Booth and Herold remained at large, John Surratt had disappeared, and even the doltish Atzerodt had eluded capture.

Atzerodt's trail should have been as easy to follow as a polecat's. In spite of Dutch courage imbibed at the Kirkwood bar on the night of the assassination, Atzerodt still lost his nerve. After a horsecar retreat out to the Washington Navy Yard, he rode the owl car back into the riotous city and stumbled into a side-street flophouse. Early Saturday morning, he walked westward out to Georgetown. There at breakfasttime he sold his Cooper revolver to a shopkeeper. Out on High Street (now Wisconsin Avenue) at 8:30 A.M., Atzerodt boarded the stagecoach for Rockville,

[58]

Maryland. In the excitement that swirled around him — horsemen galloping, couriers racing — he was conspicuous as the outgoing stage's only passenger.

On the Georgetown outskirts at Tennellytown the Army maintained a guard station. Atzerodt went through this military roadblock like a bit of flotsam drifting down a canal. True, he was detained at the guard station from 9:00 A.M. until 3:00 P.M. Then the military guards let him go!

The Army's explanation for this episode topped the pinnacle of fantasy. The soldiers admitted holding Atzerodt from morning until mid-afternoon. "During that time," read the Army's official report, "he treated the guards to several drinks and finally induced them to allow him to proceed in the wagon of one John Garther who took him as far as Rockville."

At Rockville Atzerodt burrowed into a grogshop, then spent the night somewhere in the open. That same Saturday evening the War Department identified him as one of Seward's assailants and flashed a fair description of him to police chiefs in Buffalo, Baltimore, Philadelphia, and New York. But the dispatch said he was accompanied by a heavily bearded man named "S. Thomas." Deliberate camouflage could hardly have been more misleading.

On Easter Sunday Atzerodt shambled westward to Germantown, Maryland, where he holed up with a cousin named Richter. Had he kept his mouth shut and immediately pushed on, he might easily have gained backwoods West Virginia and gone scot-free. Instead, he dillydallied for a featherbed, food, and noisy talk.

On Wednesday, April 19 (five days after Lincoln's murder), Stanton telegraphed General Hancock at Winchester: "*Atzerodt, Port Tobacco, as he is called, is known to have gone to Rockville Saturday to escape in that direction.*"

Commendation for his subsequent capture, if anyone deserved a laurel, was due Atzerodt's older brother, John, a Baltimorean serving as a Union police detective. John Atzerodt was in Lower Maryland when he heard of Lincoln's assassination. He gave Major O'Beirne a detailed description of his errant brother: "buckskin gauntlets . . . black slouch hat . . . cavalry boots with enameled leather, stitched with white. . . ." O'Beirne flashed a message to Washington advising the manhunters to scour west of Rockville.

On the evening of April 19 a cavalry detachment from Darnestown got wind of a stranger at the Richter house — a lout who said the assassins in Washington should have killed Grant, too. So the troopers snared George Atzerodt. For good measure they arrested Hartman Richter. The pair were conveyed in manacles to Washington for deposit in the iron bowels of U.S. monitor *Saugus*.

On Tuesday, April 18, Lovett led his cavalry troop to the homestead of Dr. Samuel Mudd. The doctor was out. Mrs. Mudd sent for him. Lovett questioned her while awaiting the physician. He learned that the crippled visitor at Mudd's had worn a mustache when he arrived in the night and had borrowed the doctor's razor to shave it off next day. The injured man also wore false chin whiskers of some kind, or so it appeared to Mrs. Mudd.

Dr. Mudd now returned to the house. On finding Federal cavalry there he "seemed somewhat excited," Lovett reported. He told Lieutenant Lovett that the injured man had been armed with two revolvers. When questioned further, Dr. Mudd seemed reticent about discussing the matter. Lovett gained the impression that Booth and Herold were in hiding nearby and Mudd was shielding them.

The lieutenant stationed pickets around the Mudd homestead with orders to stand watch while he himself raced back to Surrattsville to see if any more information had been wrung from tavern-keeper Lloyd.

Lovett soon returned to Dr. Mudd's farm, leading a fresh detachment of Federal cavalry. Again the doctor proved uncommunicative. Lieutenant Lovett prepared to search the house, whereupon the doctor spoke in an aside to his wife, and she went upstairs and brought down a riding boot that had been slit open. The lieutenant found the maker's name and address in the boot, and the owner's name, "*J. Wilks*." Misspelled or not,

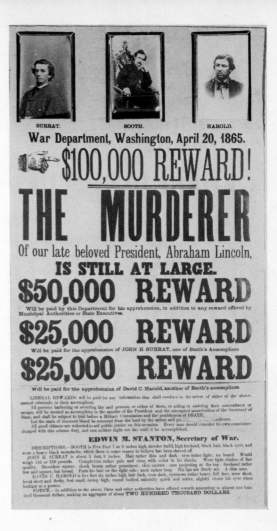

Stanton's final reward poster. (Library of Congress)

that settled it. Shown a picture of Booth, Dr. Mudd said it did not look much like the actor. With Lovett firing questions, he stated that Booth had been in his house, yes, the previous autumn. Hedging, he finally admitted that it must have been Booth whose leg he set. And he confessed to giving Booth and Herold directions to take them through Zekiah Swamp.

Lieutenant Lovett arrested Dr. Mudd forthwith and sent him under guard to Bryantown. The boot was rushed by courier to Washington. From there Colonel H. L. Burnett sent it by special messenger on a requisitioned locomotive to New York, to check with the maker on the cus-

[61]

tomer who had had it made. That night a telegram from New York City informed Burnett the boot had indeed been made for John Wilkes Booth. Burnett wrote: *"That settled the identity of the assassin in our own minds beyond all doubt."*

While that conclusion seems a little late in the day, the boot immediately convinced Washington officialdom that Dr. Mudd was criminally involved in Lincoln's murder. The unhappy physician was promptly forwarded in manacles to the national capital.

But John Wilkes Booth, David Herold, and John H. Surratt still remained at large. . . .

On Thursday, April 20, Secretary Stanton issued a proclamation calculated to produce results. This took the form of a reward poster offering $100,000 — an immense fortune in those days — for the capture of the three fugitives ($50,000 for Booth, and $25,000 each for Surratt and Herold). Eager bounty hunters also noted that the War Department promised this money *in addition to any reward offered by Municipal Authorities or State Executives."* This potential prize probably added up to the largest sweepstakes of its kind in American history.

To it, however, Secretary Stanton added: *"All persons harboring or secreting the said persons (fugitives) or aiding their concealment or escape, will be treated as accomplices in the murder of the President and subjected to the trial of a Military Commission and the punishment of DEATH."*

This decree must have sent a shudder down the Confederate underground grapevine. But even more deadly for the fugitives was the reward that turned the manhunt into a treasure hunt.

Gold Rush to Unearth Assassins—
Lafayette Baker in Action

At treasure hunting, no official on the Union side was readier to go than Secret Service Chief Baker. But Baker had not exactly been sitting on his hands since Easter. At the outset he had dug into the case, anticipating a bonanza.

Baker spread a wide dragnet. Out came "blacklists" filed in his bureau in 1863, dossiers on 13,000 or 14,000 alleged subversives. Out went Baker's agents, handcuffs ready. By April 18 seemingly endless processions of "conspiracy suspects" were marching into Old Capitol Prison or disappearing in grim military dungeons under the Winder Building. No one knows exactly how many citizens were imprisoned during this Secret Service roundup.

With significant speed Baker's agents arrested Thomas and Nannie Green, tenants of the shadowy Van Ness mansion on Seventeenth Street. A Miss Lomax, related to Nannie Green, was brought in. And a friend of Miss Lomax's, Mr. D. Preston Parr, Baltimore chinaware merchant, presumably in cahoots with John Surratt. And Clement H. Pearson, an Army lieutenant who had been seen with Booth in a Washington shooting gallery. And Benjamin Booth Cook, a dimwit arrested because of his middle name. And John R. Stolt of Chambersburg, a "suspicious character." And a circus clown who displayed Confederate money. And Dr. Francis Tumblety, a quack from Rochester, N.Y., and Brooklyn, "*arrested for complicity with Herrold* [sic]." And Oregon Wilson, a well-known Virginia artist, picked up as an associate of Tumblety's. Typically those named were seized without warrant, booked on vague charges, and held incommunicado until released at directive of Stanton, Baker, or the Old Capitol warden, jovial William P. Wood.

One of the strangest specimens hauled in by Baker's net was a Portuguese sea captain named Joao Celestino, alias Zeleste. Caught in 1864 skippering a blockade-runner out of Cuba, Celestino, paroled, had been in Washington trying to push a damages claim. On the train for Philadelphia the evening of April 14, he had been heard to say he hoped Seward would be assassinated. Baker had him picked up, ironed, and impounded in the monitor *Montauk*. Aside from Atzerodt's cousin, briefly imprisoned, Celestino was the only suspect confined in a monitor with Booth's known accomplices.

Did one of the parties hauled in by the Secret Service inform Lafayette Baker on the whereabouts of Booth and Herold? Somebody must have.

On Monday noon, April 24, Baker sat in secret session in his bureau headquarters, with his cousin Lieutenant Luther Baker, and his top scout, Lieutenant Colonel Everton Conger. The general put on an astonishing performance. For five days Booth and Herold had been somewhere in limbo. Armies of cavalry, infantry, military police, Federal scouts, detectives, deputies, and volunteers had been combing Lower Maryland without result. Now Baker spread out a map. He pointed to a spot below Port Tobacco Creek — Dent's Meadow. Here, he said, the fugitives crossed the Potomac to Virginia. Then with a drawing compass, he circled Port Conway on the Rappahannock. He told his subordinates they were to lead a cavalry squadron at top speed to that area. "*You're going after Booth,*" he told them. "*We have got a sure thing.*" Within the small circle drawn by Baker was a place called Garrett's Farm. . . .

No one knows how Baker in Washington caught the scent. A story he told afterward (that the trail was uncovered by an agent named Woodall and a nameless Negro) was exposed as a fabrication. Only recently an item researched in the National Archives threw possible light on the mystery. This was a note addressed to the War Department by a Dr. James G. Coombe. Coombe said he knew Lower Maryland and believed that Booth had been at the home of Colonel Cox. He said that Booth probably had gone from there to see Dr. Stoughten Dent near Allen's Fresh.

[64]

(Dent's Meadow on the river made the logical haven for a boat.) *"I went last night to Col. Baker,"* Coombe's note concluded, *"but I found that he was a $200,000 man & I want the Government to have the information and save the reward."*

Provost Marshal O'Beirne had already led a cavalry squadron to Port Tobacco, determined to block any chance of Booth's escape from this Rebel backwater. Scouring the region, O'Beirne got wind of someone at the Cox place carrying food to a party hiding in a nearby swamp. On Saturday, the twenty-second, he learned that two unidentified men had crossed the Potomac in a skiff.

O'Beirne went across with a detective party and scouted as far as King George's Court House. There he learned he had been chasing innocent fishermen. Or had he? Convinced Booth and Herold had gone on to Port Conway, he returned to Port Tobacco for fresh mounts. As Grant's telegraph operator had just arrived on the scene, O'Beirne sent an urgent wire asking for additional men and permission to scour the Port Conway area in Virginia. To O'Beirne's dismay, Baker bluntly ordered him to stay on the Maryland side of the Potomac.

An odd denouement concluded this episode. On Tuesday, April 25, O'Beirne in Port Tobacco received word that a man on crutches with an unkempt companion had been seen entering the swamp bottoms just north of Bryantown. Electrified, O'Beirne rushed with his troopers to that area. They found tracks in the swamp, but the fugitive couple had vanished. Evidently they were decoys. But whose? Years later Richard M. Smoot, a veteran of the Confederate underground, stated in an article that when Booth "and his party" reached Dr. Mudd's, decoys were "put in the road to make tracks. . . ." Was this second pair a bit of Baker trickery to lure O'Beirne away from the prize? The Rebel underground held no patent on such trick stratagems.

Be that as it was, O'Beirne and his troopers were diverted, and the road to fortune lay open to Lafayette Baker and company.

Dead End at Garrett's Farm

For Booth and Herold the underground road had been thorny. Their hideout in the bush at Cox's had sorely tried Booth's nerves, if the self-pitying declamations jotted down in his diary may be taken at face value.

"Wet, cold and starving, with every man's hand against me, I am here in despair, and why? For doing what Brutus was honored for, what made Tell a hero. . . ." This Shakespearean bombast sounds like Booth — still playing to the gallery, even when the audience was only a drugstore errand boy and a circle of bullfrogs.

Booth's leg doubtless badgered him in this woodland hideaway. Yet he probably exaggerated his sufferings. Every day Thomas Jones brought them a basket of food. Colonel Cox supplied brandy. These partisans also maintained a lookout for the pair in hiding. Herold probably traded them their getaway horses for this aid.

A shad fisherman, Henry Rowland, was prevailed upon by Jones to sneak a rowboat into the backwater lapping Dent's Meadow. On Friday night, April 21, Jones led the fugitives down the Potomac bluffs to the shallows near Dent's. Herold took the oars; Booth sat in the stern. They paid Jones seventeen dollars and a bottle of whiskey. Herold shoved off.

In the misty dark on the broad channel Herold took an oblique tangent, rowing upstream toward Nanjemoy Creek. Most historians assume this was a time-consuming error. Actually Herold may have been seeking a blockade-runner's yawl or cutter in the Port Tobacco inlet. If so, he sweated out a futile row.

They hid out the following day in junglelike Nanjemoy Cove. Federal gunboats steamed down the Potomac channel, pacing troops who combed the riverbank. After dark, Herold pushed off again. Hard rowing and luck carried the skiff over to Mathias Point.

On this Sunday, April 23, Herold guided Booth to the farmhouse of a Mrs. Quesenberry. Nervously this lady relayed him to the home of Dr. Richard Stewart, reputedly the richest man in the county and an avowed

The Garrett farmhouse, and the porch where Booth died. House is no longer standing. (Rare photo courtesy Miss Elizabeth Winslow and Miss Edna Zuber, author's collection)

Confederate sympathizer. But Stewart's sympathies, it appeared, did not embrace an assassin marked with a death decree for harboring. He fed the fugitives, then passed them on to the backwoods cabin of a Negro, William Lucas. Infuriated, the race-conscious Booth sent Stewart five dollars with a caustic note: "*I cannot blame you for your want of hospitality . . . but . . . I needed medical assistance . . . I would not have turned a dog away from my door in such a plight. . . .*" He repaid Lucas for his hospitality by ousting him and his wife from the cabin.

Early Monday morning Lucas conveyed the two men in a springer wagon to Port Conway on the Rappahannock. The fugitives paid Lucas ten dollars and sat down to wait for the ferry to Port Royal on the opposite bank. Three Confederate cavalrymen came along. They said they were veterans of Mosby's disbanded regiment. Herold beckoned them aside for a whispered conversation. A trooper named Willie Jett volunteered to guide the fugitives to the home of Richard Garrett, a couple of miles south of Port Royal. On the road Booth shared Jett's horse.

At Garrett's Farm near Bowling Green, about seventy-eight miles from Washington, the homestead under the locust trees offered sanctuary. Jett introduced Booth as "John W. Boyd," one of Lee's soldiers wounded

[67]

in the Richmond campaign. Richard Garrett set a table for the visitors. Booth remained that night with the Garretts while Herold found quarters in Bowling Green.

Tuesday morning Herold rejoined Booth. They spent the day lounging on the farmhouse porch, chatting with the Garrett boys and Miss L. K. B. Holloway, a schoolteacher residing with the family. Then a cloud darkened the bucolic scene. At evening one of the Confederate cavalrymen dashed past the dooryard at full gallop. He warned Booth that "Bluebellies" were crossing the Rappahannock at Port Conway.

A squadron of Federal cavalry came up the road, heading for Bowling Green. To Farmer Garrett's dismay, his two guests raced into a pine thicket behind his barn. This rush to hide worried the Garretts. William, the elder of two sons, went to a neighboring farm to inquire into the Federal cavalry parade. When he returned some time later that evening, he told the two fugitives who had emerged from the wood that they must move on in the morning, so as not to make serious trouble for his father.

Disturbed by Booth's demeanor and dark remarks he had made about going to Mexico, William Garrett and Miss Holloway decided the armed pair were desperadoes who might steal the family's horses. So occurred one of the strangest episodes of the entire drama. At bedtime (as Miss Holloway recalled it) Booth refused to sleep in the house. At this William Garrett conducted Booth and Herold to the tobacco barn in the side yard. The outbuilding housed stored furniture packed in straw. The unwelcome guests were told they could sleep in this jumble. Then, by way of protecting his father's stable, William Garrett locked the visitors in!

The curtain was now cued to fall on the ill-starred career of John Wilkes Booth.

Of course Lafayette Baker based his calculations on the gratuitous information from Dr. Coombe and an intelligence tap on O'Beirne's wire to General Augur. For the cavalry detail the Secret Service chief obtained twenty-five troopers of the Sixteenth New York Volunteer Cavalry under Lieutenant Edward P. Doherty. Lieutenant Colonel Con-

[68]

ger rode in honorary command as former leader of "Baker's Rangers." Lieutenant Luther Baker, the chief's cousin, had the expedition's field command.

The troopers went by Potomac steamer *Ide* to Belle Plain, a river landing to the west of Mathias Point. From there they raced to King George's Court House, then down to Port Conway. The Negro ferryman on duty, William Rollins, informed them a cripple on crutches accompanied by a younger man and three Rebel cavalrymen had crossed to Port Royal.

In Port Royal the Rebel trooper who gave Booth a lift was identified as Willie Jett, a lad visiting Bowling Green. Full speed ahead, Doherty's "Blue-bellies" went racing on down to Bowling Green to hunt for Jett. Around midnight they trapped him at the home of his fiancée. With a gun at his head, he talked.

With Jett in tow, Luther Baker, Conger, and Doherty rushed a cavalry raid on Garrett's farm. They reached the place about 3:30 A.M. Leaving the horses in blocking position down the road, they crept up on the house, Indian fashion. Doherty hammered on the door. When Richard Garrett appeared in nightshirt, candle in hand, he was seized unceremoniously by Lieutenant Baker, who demanded to know Booth's whereabouts. Terrified, the farmer swore that "Boyd" and his friend had fled to the woods.

His spluttering sounded untruthful. So Baker and Conger forced him to mount a stump under a locust tree and threatened to hang him unless he talked. At this, William and young Jack Garrett, who had been sleeping in a corncrib in order to guard their father's horses, came running forward. William pointed out the tobacco barn as Booth's hiding place. Doherty immediately deployed his cavalrymen around the barn. Baker and Conger ordered the fugitives to drop their guns.

At once a dialogue began between the Federal officers and the quarry trapped in the barn. For perhaps twenty minutes Colonel Conger and Luther Baker argued, urging Booth to surrender. From the dark barn a voice shouted refusal, then appealed "give a lame man a show," and

In this illustration from Harper's Weekly *of 1865, John Wilkes Booth is shown burning in the tobacco barn of Garrett's Farm. (Author's collection)*

finally offered to shoot it out with the soldiers if they would duel with him in single combat.

Impatient with all this, Conger ordered the fugitives to give up, or else the barn would be torched. Whereupon David Herold wailed that he wanted to get out. This evoked a string of epithets from his companion. After more recriminations, Herold was told to thrust his hands out of the door as soon as it was unlocked. A moment later the door was set ajar; Herold's pale hands appeared in the gloom.

Conger caught the wrists in an iron grasp, and Herold was yanked from the barn. Blue cavalrymen pinioned him and dragged him away from the barn. As the soldiers surrounded him he began to whimper, begging for mercy. Herold told Conger he had no part in the assassination; he "always liked Mr. Lincoln's jokes." Angrily Conger ordered him tied to a tree.

Luther Baker and Doherty continued to urge their quarry to come out of the barn, with his hands up. Booth then began a diatribe about "staining the glorious old banner." Determined to end this, Colonel Conger decided to fire the barn. Typical of these tobacco barns, it was loosely boarded with planks spaced about three inches apart to admit air. Conger dodged to the building's rear, touched a match to a fistful of straw, and thrust it through a gap in the planking.

At once a wave of fire billowed across the bone-dry mow, and the barn's interior came to view in a flush of crimson light. Exposed in the glare, a figure on crutches stood facing the door, a carbine clasped to his breast. As the Federal troopers watched fascinated from the darkness outside, the melodramatic actor dropped his carbine, snatched up a small table, and wheeled as though to fight the hot blaze.

Lieutenant Doherty had been enjoined by strict War Department orders to take Booth alive. He had ordered his cavalry troopers to hold their fire and shoot only as a last resort. Now, as the man in the barn dropped the useless table and rounded toward the door, apparently drawing a pistol, a shot cracked out above the roar of the blaze. The victim in the barn pitched forward on his crutches and fell flat on his face.

At once, Luther Baker plunged into the burning building, grabbed the revolver from the man's spasmodic clutch, and wrestled the inert body outside. Conger came around the side of the barn to lend a hand. As they stood over the body, Conger asked Baker why he had shot the captured fugitive. Baker stared at Conger, then said: *"I thought you shot him!"* Doherty walked up, wearing a baffled expression. Hadn't Booth committed suicide? The three officers stared at one another blankly.

Due to strange gaps and contradictory hedging in the formal testimony, no senatorial inquest or ultimate historical inquiry could determine exactly what happened that night at Garrett's Farm. But it seemed that a cavalry sergeant came forward to assert that he had shot the captive. Asked why he had done it against orders, he said God had told him to. He also

Sergeant Boston Corbett, the psychotic Union soldier who claimed that he shot Booth. (National Archives)

added that he wanted to prevent possible loss of life among the cavalrymen. *"I braced my weapon across my arm, aimed through a crack in the timbering and shot him."*

The sergeant's fellow troopers hooted when they heard this claim. No one among them had witnessed the shot. And the man who said he fired it was a former street-corner evangelist who had also been an insane-asylum inmate — Sergeant Boston Corbett, known to the Sixteenth New York as "Glory to God" Boston.

Still wrangling over who had fired the shot, the officers ordered the fallen man carried to the front porch of the Garrett house. He was obviously dying, and in great agony. Examination showed he had been hit in the nape of the neck by a shot similar to the one that had struck Lincoln. However, the ball had severed the spinal column, causing a most agonizing wound.

Brandy was administered. A doctor was sent for. And the dying man was searched. From his person the Federals took a briar pipe, a file, a Bowie knife, two revolvers, a compass, a Canadian bank draft, a diamond pin, and a diary. Due to freakish military censorship, these items would

[72]

later cause controversy. As articles of evidence, they should have gone under guard to Washington. Instead, only some reached official hands. Others eventually disappeared.

The pipe, for instance, ended up as a curio in a saloon in far-off Rochester, New York. The diamond stickpin vanished. Baker and Conger itemized the meager Canadian bill of exchange, but years later the Confederate undergrounder Richard M. Smoot published a seemingly reliable statement that Booth had carried $6,500 in U.S. currency on his person when he fled Washington — a sum lost somewhere in the shuffle? In a pocket of Booth's diary the Federals found the photographs of five women, all intimate friends of Booth. Four were actresses. The fifth picture drew the War Department designation of a "well-known Washington society woman." As late as 1952 this lady's name was withheld from publication out of deference to her family. Such rank favoritism typified military censorship. Yet the fact remained that Bessie Hale, daughter of Senator Hale, was secretly engaged to John Wilkes Booth and may have known a great deal about his conspiratorial activities.

The signet ring Booth always wore was not listed by his captors. Was it on the dying man dragged from the barn? Certainly it would have aided in his identification. No mention of it was made by the officers at Garrett's. Nor were the captive's pistols and carbine subjected to examination. Official inspection of these weapons might have settled the question of the fatal shot.

Nor were Sergeant Corbett's side arms inspected. Significantly he stated that he fired a revolver at Booth. Yet a few days after the cavalry squad returned to Washington, Secretary Stanton wrote a requisition asking that a service revolver be issued to Sergeant Boston Corbett.

The Missing Diary

But it was Booth's diary that was to pose the big question mark. This little notebook and some of his other effects were rushed to Washington by Colonel Conger, who swung into the saddle and took off before the captive on the farmhouse porch expired. At 5:00 P.M. of that Wednesday Conger burst into Lafayette Baker's office with the news that Booth had been trapped and shot. Elated, the Secret Service chief rushed off with Conger to tell Stanton. Among other items, the diary was handed to the war secretary.

Stanton kept the diary overnight, then turned it over to Major T. T. Eckert, his code and cipher specialist. Eckert locked it in a War Department safe. Months later, when it came to light, examiners discovered that eighteen pages preceding the night of the assassination had been cut out. Stanton said he knew nothing about it. And Eckert, soon to become a general, said he knew nothing about the excised pages. If the diary had had anything significant to say, its posthumous voice was effectively silenced.

The voice of the dying captive seems to have been silenced, too. Conger and Luther Baker were presumably adept at interrogation. But if anyone asked the expiring man any questions about the assassination conspiracy, the answers were never recorded. The officers asked if he wanted brandy. Could he swallow? He was able to moan replies. Conger hadn't waited. And the words finally put in the dying man's mouth were fictionalized utterances to his mother and patriotic platitudes for public recital.

Miss Holloway had come out of the house to administer to the dying man as best she could. The Garrett boys looked on, enthralled. Roosters crowed. The fiery barn collapsed. A Dr. Urquhart arrived on the scene. Bending over the victim, he shook his head. The man gasped, "Water!" He could not swallow, but Miss Holloway moistened his lips with a damp cloth. The deathwatch dragged on.

A soldier witness noticed that the dying captive wore "a gray woolen

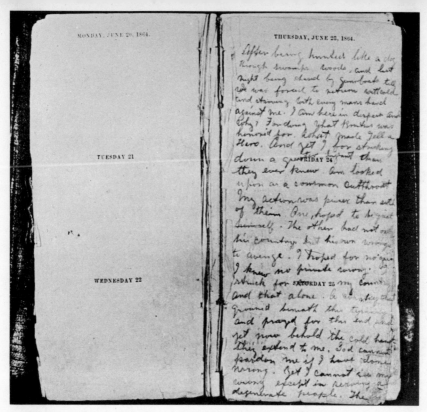

A page from Booth's diary. Note that the printed dates are almost a year before the assassination. Booth apparently wrote indiscriminately on whatever free page he could find in a blank diary. (National Park Service)

shirt; dark cassimere pants; one cavalry, or theater, top boot which drew up above the knees [sic] but was turned down when captured. On the other foot he had an old shoe." Inexplicably Lieutenant Luther Baker paid no notice to his prisoner's clothes, and they elicited no War Department mention. This oversight, if so it was, had to be remarkable in that Booth was a known spy. And the Secret Service officers would have been acutely aware that Rebel agents frequently concealed maps in the lining of their garments, might wear tiny code-picture "minicam" tintypes in the form of buttons, and carried rice-paper messages in hollow-heeled boots. Perhaps the officers at Garrett's were so preoccupied with thoughts of the reward money that they regarded the captive in a gold-blinded daze.

The two tense lieutenants, Baker and Doherty, waited for their prize catch to die. He begged them to kill him. They stared at him stonily. Pale sunlight was dissolving the morning mist when an end came to the excruciating death struggle.

Time: About seven in the morning of Wednesday, April 26. Exit John Wilkes Booth. The public was told that Lincoln's assassination was now avenged.

Conspiracy Conclusion

The conspiracy trial that condemned Booth's accomplices evolved as a judicial parody. The Military Trial Commission was headed by Army General Joseph Holt and directed by Secretary Stanton behind the scenes. The Army tribunal — six generals and two colonels — composed a group of stern Cromwells disposed to convict. The trial opened on May 9, 1865, just three weeks after the arrest of Mrs. Surratt. Several of the defendants had been unable to procure lawyers in that short a time; the attorneys procurable had been given no opportunity to study evidence briefs, obtain friendly witnesses, or prepare any sort of case.

The mass indictment was a complicated affair involving eight defendants. In this proceeding, devised by Judge Holt's Bureau of Military Justice under Stanton's eye, John Surratt was named number-one conspirator and indicted *in absentia*. Paine, Herold, Atzerodt, Dr. Mudd, Spangler, Arnold, O'Laughlin, and Mary Surratt were charged with *"combining, confederating and conspiring, together with . . . Jefferson Davis . . . and others unknown . . . to kill and murder within the Military Department of Washington . . . Abraham Lincoln . . . and lying in wait . . . with intent . . . to kill . . . Andrew Johnson . . . and . . . Ulysses S. Grant. . . ."*

Obviously this blanket indictment was full of holes. *Prima facie* evi-

[76]

dence would show that Dr. Mudd had been "lying in wait" to kill nobody when the fugitives woke him at four o'clock in the morning after the assassination. Neither had Mrs. Surratt "lain in wait" to murder anyone.

The prisoners (Mrs. Surratt excepted) clanked into court at the Arsenal Penitentiary in chains. With the exception of Dr. Mudd, all the men had been cruelly tortured at Stanton's explicit order, and alleged confessions had been extracted under extreme duress. For civilian counsel the military court proceedings proved a nightmare. Every objection raised by the defense was overruled. Every point for the prosecution was granted. The volunteer defender for Mrs. Surratt, Maryland's brilliant Reverdy Johnson, was rudely insulted and squelched; he quit the case when Holt raised the issue of a loyalty oath. General Sherman's brother-in-law, General Thomas Ewing, defending Mudd, Arnold, and Spangler, and Major W. E. Doster, for Paine and Atzerodt, were thwarted at every turn. So was Herold's counsel.

On June 30 all eight defendants were found guilty of subversive participation in the assassination conspiracy. Dr. Mudd, Samuel Arnold, and Michael O'Laughlin received life sentences. Edward Spangler drew six years. Lewis Paine, David Herold, George Atzerodt, and Mary Eugenia Surratt were sentenced to hang.

Despite the drumhead trial proceedings, death sentences for Paine, Herold, and Atzerodt seemed merited enough. But nobody believed Mrs. Surratt would actually go to the gallows. Strenuous efforts were made to have her sentence commuted. Dozens of Northern liberals spoke up in her behalf. And not all of the Army tribunal were kangaroo hangmen. Generals Hunter, Foster, Kautz, and Ekin, and Colonel Tompkins signed a petition recommending clemency. Judge Holt was supposed to deliver this clemency petition to President Andrew Johnson. Afterward Johnson stated he never saw or heard of it. But Secretary Stanton wanted Mrs. Surratt to hang and he said so.

Thus, on the morning of July 7, 1865 — barely ten weeks after the shooting at Garrett's Farm and only twenty-four hours after President Johnson signed the death warrants — Mrs. Surratt, Lewis Paine, David

[77]

Four of the conspirators condemned and hanged. Left to right on the gallows are Mary Surratt, Lewis Paine, David Herold, and George Atzerodt. (Library of Congress)

Herold, and George Atzerodt marched to the gallows in the yard of the Arsenal Penitentiary.

After the multiple hanging, *New York World* journalist George Alfred Townsend wrote: "*This court was needed to show us at least the petty tyranny of martial law and the pettiness of military jurists.*" But the malfeasances in the conspiracy trial surpassed any misdemeanor "pettiness." Months later it was discovered that the War Department and Secret Service fabricated evidence, faked "captured" documents, and suborned witnesses in a notorious "perjury school" in an effort to implicate certain Confederate leaders in the assassination. This fakery merely watered down and weakened the actual case against the Richmond Government, which undoubtedly approved Lincoln's murder as a "military assassination" mission. That is if the Rains agent who warned Lincoln spoke the truth.

In its haste to convict Booth's accomplices, the Bureau of Military Justice bypassed some important suspects. The Greens of the Van Ness mansion on Seventeenth Street — Preston Parr of Baltimore — weird Dr. Tumblety — Joao Celestino — why were these known subversives freed? Why did Colonel Cox and Thomas Jones, who harbored Booth and Herold for six days, go scot-free? And what of John F. Parker, the guard who deserted his post at Lincoln's box? Why did he go unpunished?

When Stanton died in 1869, reportedly by suicide, there were buried with him the answers to a whole arcanum of mysteries. Why, although indicted as the number-one conspirator, was John H. Surratt never brought to justice? Stanton deliberately permitted his escape. When Superintendent Richards' police squad tracked Surratt to Montreal and thence to Trois Rivières, Canada, Stanton summarily stopped the chase and ordered the detective party home. He then incarcerated Louis Wiechmann; severely reprimanded Richards for pursuing Surratt; refused to act when Surratt was next reported in Liverpool, England; canceled the reward when a ship's doctor claimed it for identifying the fugitive; remained silent when the U.S. Consul General in Rome reported Surratt's enlistment as a Zouave in the Papal Guard, and made no move when Surratt fled Italy. When finally arrested in Cairo and returned to the States at the behest of Secretary Seward, John Surratt won a mistrial in 1867 and then was freed by the statute of limitations. Why was this miscarriage of justice allowed? What shielded this indicted murder accomplice?

Perhaps such questions should have been addressed to the ghost of Lafayette Baker, who died, aged forty-four, in Philadelphia in 1868. He also left a book of puzzles behind him. One of the blackest concerned a rumor that Lincoln's assassination was a Vatican plot. It was alleged Booth died clutching a scapular medal (a Catholic medallion), and that all the conspirators were Catholics. This fabrication came from the brain of Secret Service Chief Baker.

Characteristically, this "plot" was wholesale mendacity containing a semblance of truth to make it plausible. That is, Mrs. Surratt, John Surratt, and Dr. Mudd were Catholics. But John Wilkes Booth was, if anything, a nominal Episcopalian. Lewis Paine was reared a hardshell Baptist. Herold and Arnold were Episcopalians. Atzerodt's family had been Lutheran. Spangler was apparently nothing. And Michael O'Laughlin's family seem to have been Methodists. As for Booth's scapular, the Garrett family (Baptist Fundamentalist) flatly contradicted the tale.

But like poison ivy, the story took root. For a century it was peddled in the American South. It was even whispered as a smear during John Kennedy's presidential campaign; the radical California "Minutemen" distributed leaflets telling the stale old libel — "the Catholics murdered Abraham Lincoln" — and it may also have influenced Lee Harvey Oswald's trigger finger.

The Nazis, too, concocted their own version of a Lincoln conspiracy fantasy. In this fabrication, Lincoln's murder was a Jewish plot devised by Paris bankers who had been angered by Lincoln's inflationary "greenback policy." Booth was supposed to have been a Rothschild hireling, and "atheistic money-lenders" were alleged to have paid Booth's way to Canada for "pistol practice." Actually, Booth had been a crack shot since boyhood. Also, as a youth he had joined the anti-Catholic, anti-Jewish "Know Nothing" party. So much for the Nazi version.

[80]

The conspirator who got away. John Surratt in the uniform of a Papal Zouave. (Library of Congress)

The U.S. War Department could have easily refuted the original "Vatican plot" libel. Instead, it was swept under the rug. Embarrassed by Baker's chicanery, later officials went so far as to deny that the U.S. Secret Service even existed during the Civil War. Further, witnessing news correspondents and an account by McKinley's Secret Service guard to the contrary, it was officially asserted as late as the Eisenhower Administration that the Secret Service had not been assigned to protect the President's person until after President McKinley's assassination in 1901.

Although previous attempts on American Presidents had been reported, Lincoln was the first United States President to be assassinated. The subsequent assassination of Presidents Garfield, McKinley, and Kennedy; murderous attacks on Theodore Roosevelt, Franklin D. Roosevelt, and Truman; the recent killing of prominent Negro leaders and social reformers climaxed by the murder of Martin Luther King and Senator Robert Kennedy — these successive crimes have led various commentators to conclude that the veneer of law and order and civilized behavior is

[81]

markedly thin in the United States of America. Indeed, some critics aver that the nation exists on the surface of a volcanic substrata of criminality ready at any moment to erupt and inundate the country in waves of sedition and rampant homicide.

Any comprehensive examination of history must reveal the fallacy of such a view. Every great war has beset society with an aftermath of lawlessness, and assassination is a crime by no means indigenous to the United States. The very word "assassin" derives from an Arabic term meaning "eater of hashish." It was originally applied in the eleventh century to Persian, Syrian, and other Moslem fanatics committed to the killing of Crusaders.

Thus it remains peculiarly apt as concerns the slaying of public leaders or activists dedicated to ethical concepts of government or to drastic social reform. Long before the founding of the American Republic, Europe was drenched by the blood of assassination victims. The early religious wars, the French Revolution, the Napoleonic Wars, stained Western world history with assassinations.

Lincoln's murder was soon followed by the killing of liberal Czar Alexander. Numerous Russian, Austrian, German, and Middle European statesmen were slain in the closing years of the nineteenth century. A powder train of similar homicides led up to the Balkans killings, the probable slaying of inventor Rudolf Diesel, the Serajevo assassination, and the murder of France's leading Socialist — crimes that triggered off World War I.

The Russian Revolution of 1917 produced an anthology of assassinations. Then, in the wake of the 1918 Armistice, German militarists slew leftist leaders Rosa Luxemburg and Karl Liebknecht. In Ireland the desperate I.R.A. unleashed an assassination campaign. Again the Balkans exploded, bringing death to such leaders as Stephen Raditch and King Alexander of Yugoslavia. During these decades assassinations were rife in Central and South American countries. In Mexico endemic assassinations had cost the lives of several presidents and brave peasant leader Zapata.

In the 1930's, assassination bloodbaths swamped Stalinist Russia,

Fascist Italy and Spain, Nazi Germany, militarist Japan. Deplorable as it remains, the American record pales in comparison with these last, which occurred, one might note, in military domains and police states that exercised iron disciplines. Obviously government by army forces and secret police may do as much to incite or abet assassinations as does revolutionary lawlessness.

However, to point a finger at Stalinist Russia, say, or Hitler Germany merely indulges a psychological "transference of guilt," certainly unwarranted of a country with a homicide record that embraces Western gunslinging, Prohibition gang wars, Ku Klux terrorism, such crimes as the unpunished slaying of Medgar Evers, and the murder of four Presidents. Yet Europe's military dictatorships do indicate that stern rule and regimentation were not the answer to law and order; in fact, military establishments have themselves sponsored assassinations since the days of the Spanish Inquisition and Britain's Oliver Cromwell.

Which brings up the point that the motives behind the crime are various and often hidden — compulsions may range from holier-than-thou religious mania, tribal feuding, or vendetta vengeance, to rabid racism, superpatriotism, or back-hall politics. The assassin may be a lone wolf, a secret agent on mission, a hired killer, a trained soldier, or a mad fanatic.

In an effort to capsule the problem, a recent U.S. Secret Service chief asserted that all the assassins who struck down American Presidents were insane. Were this true, the U.S. Government would obviously stand guilty of condemning men who had not been responsible for their actions. The insanity contention also serves to screen the motivation of a Booth who operated as a secret agent and was probably committed to a "military assassination" mission. Nor is the crime less reprehensible when garbed, as was Booth's, in the political costume of a Brutus role. Be the killer a soldier or an operative in a conspiratorial underground, the assassin remains a red-handed murderer operating beyond the law. Manifestly no society can tolerate the individual or group that secretly endows itself with the powers of star-chamber judge and executioner.

[83]

It seems evident that such a secret group worked behind the scenes to support the assassination strike in Washington on the night of April 14, 1865. Equally evident is the fact that all of the guilty were never brought to justice. Booth spoke of fifty accomplices; Herold said thirty-five.

At any rate, a pamphlet issued in the 1940's by the Medical Museum of the Armed Forces Institute of Pathology states: *"Confusion and mystery still surround the shooting of Abraham Lincoln, and we will probably never know all the facts. One thing is sure . . . his murder was part of a large conspiracy. . . ."* — a fact hushed up at the time.

And another thing is sure. Abraham Lincoln was not murdered by Vatican agents, international hirelings, or foreigners of any stamp. Abraham Lincoln was murdered by his fellow Americans — some of those who had been indicted, and some labeled simply as "others unknown."

Bibliography

Baker, Gen. Lafayette C., *History of the United States Secret Service* (Philadelphia: privately published, 1867).

Bates, David Homer, *Lincoln in the Telegraph Office* (New York: D. Appleton-Century Co., 1907).

Beyer, Wm. Gilmore, *On Hazardous Service* (New York: Harper & Brothers, 1912).

Buckingham, J. E., Sr., *Reminiscenses and Souvenirs of the Assassination of Abraham Lincoln* (Washington, D.C.: Rufus Darby, 1894).

Crook, Wm., *Through Five Administrations* (New York: Harper & Brothers, 1907).

DeWitt, David M., *The Assassination of Lincoln and Its Expiation* (New York: Macmillan, 1909).

Eisenschiml, Otto, *Why Was Lincoln Murdered?* (New York: Grosset & Dunlap, 1937).

Grant, Hamil, *Spies and Secret Service* (New York: Stokes, 1915).

Harris, Gen. T. M., *Assassination of Lincoln, a History of the Great Conspiracy* (Boston: American Citizen Co., 1892).

Jones, Thos. A., *John Wilkes Booth* (Chicago: Laird and Lee, 1897).

Kimmel, Stanley, *The Mad Booths of Maryland* (New York: Bobbs-Merrill, 1940).

Laughlin, Clara E., *The Death of Lincoln; The Story of Booth's Plot, His Deed and the Penalty* (New York: Doubleday, Page & Co., 1909).

Mudd, Nettie (Ed.), *The Life of Dr. Samuel A. Mudd* (New York: Neale Pub. Co., 1906).

Oldroyd, O. H., *The Assassination of Abraham Lincoln* (Washington, D.C.: privately published, 1901).

Pinkerton, Allan, *Spy of the Rebellion* (New York: G. W. Carleton & Co., 1883).

Pitman, Benn, *The Assassination of President Lincoln and Trial of the Conspirators* (Cincinnati: Moore, Wilsatch & Baldwin, 1865).

Pratt, Fletcher, *Stanton, Lincoln's Secretary of War* (New York: W. W. Norton, 1953).

Roscoe, Theodore, *The Web of Conspiracy* (Englewood Cliffs: Prentice-Hall, 1959).

Sandburg, Carl, *Abraham Lincoln, the War Years*, Vol. IV (New York: Harcourt, Brace & Co., 1939).

Skinner, Otis, *The Mad Folk of the Theater* (Indianapolis: Bobbs-Merrill, 1928).

Smoot, R. M., *The Unwritten History of the Assassination of Abraham Lincoln* (Baltimore: John Murphy Co., 1904).

Starr, John W. Jr., *Lincoln's Last Day* (New York: Stokes, 1922).

Stern, Philip Van Doren, *The Man Who Killed Lincoln* (New York: Literary Guild, 1939).

Townsend, Geo. Alfred, *The Life, Crime and Capture of J. W. Booth* (New York: Dick & Fitzgerald, 1865).

Wilson, Francis, *John Wilkes Booth* (Boston and New York: Houghton Mifflin, 1928).

Index

[87]

[88]

Surratt, John, 5, 14, 16, 19, 20, 22, 23, 76, 79, 80
   See also Manhunt
Surratt, Mrs. Mary, 5, 14-23, 24, 25, 39, 76, 77, 80
   capture of, 57
   See also Manhunt
Surrattsville, 5, 14, 19, 24, 26, 39, 45, 50, 52, 60

Taft, Dr. Charles, 31
Tanner, James, 43, 44
Townsend, George Alfred, quoted, 79
Turner, Ella, 16

Tyrell, Lt., 42

Van Alen, James, 5-6

Warne, Mrs. Kate. *See* Pinkerton agents
Welles, Gideon, 31
Wiechmann, Louis J., 4, 16, 18, 22, 24, 25
   See also Manhunt
Williams, William, 55
Withers, Jr., William, 30
Wood, Reverend. *See* Powell, Lewis Thornton
Wood, William P., 9, 63